T0128438

Being Rebuilt & Restored

Your life's a building process—living stones being restored into
His eternal kingdom and presence. How God is busy
transforming your rubble site into His holy dwelling place.

ANJA BRONKHORST

WESTBOW
PRESS®
A DIVISION OF THOMAS NELSON
& ZONDERVAN

WestBow Press books may be ordered through booksellers or by contacting:

WestBow Press
A Division of Thomas Nelson & Zondervan
1663 Liberty Drive
Bloomington, IN 47403
www.westbowpress.com
1 (866) 928-1240

ISBN: 978-1-9736-5717-0 (sc)
ISBN: 978-1-9736-5716-3 (hc)
ISBN: 978-1-9736-5718-7 (e)

Library of Congress Control Number: 2019903177

Print information available on the last page.

WestBow Press rev. date: 4/04/2019

I dedicate this book foremost and ultimately to my Heavenly Father, the Master Architect of this extraordinary life and the one beyond. Everything is from You, about You, and for You. I fervently pray that every word contributes to building Your kingdom and repairing many broken walls.

This book is for every reader and every person out there, building and sweating through the hard labour of temporary life—may you receive a new grace-filled spiritual perspective to endure until the final revealing day!

Contents

PART 1
GROUND, PLAN, AND FOUNDATION

PART 2
STRUCTURE

PART 3
FINISHING TOUCHES AND MAINTENANCE

PART 1
GROUND, PLAN, AND FOUNDATION

Introduction

Do you also hear it? The silence...

An uncomfortable, aching silence. So painful that the silence is actually screaming, cutting in somewhere between marrow and bone, body and soul. The crying absence of God's original design—for humanity, families, relationships, and every individual person—for yourself...

Do you also see it? The dust hanging in front of your eyes, a hazy reality of the condition or environment you currently find yourself in.

Too much building rubble everywhere you look...

What was once breathtakingly beautiful and glorious, lays in ruins.

Broken.

The screaming silence competes with the noise of all the other forms of brokenness around you. Every person hears it and is affected by it, but few really listen or truly understand.

Your inner being screams—with or without words. The soul speaks a complicated language, and the spirit understands. And the body can't help but demonstrate this ongoing dialogue. Broken from the inside out— desperate for repair and order, for some form of relief!

Tears mix with the dirt and dust. Through the muddy tears, everything looks distorted, damaged, and disordered. Messy.

Where tears have dried up, dry cracks have formed—urgently requiring moisture, living water—life! To those who can't or refuse to cry, desperate and pleading for softening and mending yet challenging and merciless at the same time.

The footprints of the enemy lay visibly and unapologetic around the scene. Loyal to his nature of deception, his footprints are mixed with your own ánd those who have walked here before you.

The feeling of abandonment clings closer to your core than your own sweat to your exhausted limbs.

The destruction of the gloriously beautiful scene—of hope— activates something within you. There's something inside of you that wants to fight and protest. It's more complicated than rebellion and deeper than consciousness that spurs into action. To humbly stumble into action...

Seeking answers. Seeking the next step. To close your eyes won't help anymore. The damage isn't disappearing. To the contrary, the weeds among the building rubble are actually overgrowing and flourishing ferociously. The renovation required to fix the damage, only really intensifies with time. The longer you try to look away, the louder the scene is calling to be heard. The longer you wait, the bigger the built-up frustration grows. Those who truly listen and understand, can't help but to respond.

How did this happen, God? What part did we play in this? What did You want from me? What *do* You want from me? I'm sorry, God...

Do You even hear me...?

Answering the Call to Restore

God, I lie before You—broken and bare
I sense Your powerful presence: the first touch of repair
But I'm ashamed of my nakedness
And offering to You not beauty, but a total mess...
God, they say You can bring beauty from ashes
But I feel blinded by these dusty lashes
Does that really apply to me?
Please help me sincerely see...
God, they say Your Word is alive and relevant;
The stories and characters still applicable to the present
I've come to my end and surrender all control
I confess:
I alone, cannot fix this mess...
I willingly open my hands and heart
To Your Holy Spirit, to be set apart
Please renew and restore me –
All for Your kingdom
And Your Glory
Amen.

Chapter 1

Your Gap in the Wall

*But instead we will remain strong and always sincere in our love
as we express the truth. All our direction and ministries will flow
from Christ and lead us deeper into him, the anointed Head of
his body, the church. For his "body" has been formed in his image
and is closely joined together and closely connected as one. And
every member has been given divine gifts to **contribute to the
growth of all**; and as these gifts operate effectively throughout
the whole body, **we are built up and made perfect in love.***
—*Ephesians 4:15–16 (TPT)*

As you are looking at the building rubble, you are becoming
aware of something that you've never really seen before. At
times there has just been so much dust, wind, and resistance that
you've never really noticed it. Now, what you see, can never be
unseen: the big gap.

The massive gap inside of your heart. The massive gap that you
are sitting in. The massive gap in the rest of the wall—the empty
space you are leaving in somebody else's life. It's not only the
absence of your presence but also the absence of your function—
the absence of your purpose and your calling. This gap, that you've
always experienced as your own lot to carry and to fix. An open
breach you've always subconsciously tried to hide and disguise
with other worldly available building material, covered up by

temporary, insufficient structures. This big gap within a life that longs for fulfilment and meaning. It's no wonder it hurts so much and feels so uncomfortable; it needs urgent attention!

You weren't prepared for this—that the image of the big gap would look worse and uglier than the entire rubble site. It might even have been better for you when the dust was chaotically blazing about, hindering your clear vision. Maybe you even desire to take a step backwards in this transformational process. In a way, it may have been easier to aimlessly drift about the chaotic construction site than to come to a halt and make up-close contact with it in all its truth.

Now you can see things that can never be erased from your mind, and you realise the truth that those who gain knowledge really do gain sorrow. Repentance goes hand in hand with sorrow. It's bittersweet, for a lack of knowledge also destroys lives. You don't want to process this hurt, but you also don't want a destroyed life. There has to be a way to use this knowledge for restorative purposes, even if the process entails a lot of pain and unease.

The uncomfortable reality that settles in and will never leave you again is that you now carry a responsibility for this big gap. A wall with a gap is meaningless and insufficient. It also threatens to cause the rest of the building around it to crack and collapse.

You've never really thought about it that way. You've always been convinced by the lies of the enemy that your gap is rather insignificant and doesn't really have a big influence. The truth is that wholeness is only real in unity. If you choose to build your own little tower, with your own stones, in your own way, next to the entire building, avoiding the discomfort of being touched or influenced by other living stones, you might be missing the whole reason for your existence.

You were created to fill a special piece of the entire unity— to *receive* support and also to *provide* support. By withdrawing yourself, you are not only limiting the reaching of your own purpose and potential, but others' potential as well. We are all living stones being built together into a spiritual house (1 Peter 2:5). Although you might feel discouraged by the amount of work that lies ahead, you will soon understand and appreciate that you are not alone in this process.

Like in the days of Biblical figures Zerubbabel, Ezra and Nehemiah, we are finding ourselves again in a time of a broken temple and broken city walls. The broken temple represents God's broken children, and the broken city walls represent the broken unity of families, marriages, and relationships of believers. A broken body of believers. A broken society.

God's children are currently released from the enemy's enslavement, just like God's chosen people were released from their captivity in Babylonia. Though free, the Jews were rather passive, emotionally drained, and spiritually bent. There was no passion, planning, or leadership to repair the broken walls of Jerusalem, their holy city. This incredibly special and holy place of worship was where they have encountered God's manifest presence. Many Jews even chose not to return to their broken-down home and nation but rather preferred to live among their enemies. To some, it might have seemed easier to continue with the by then familiar oppressed circumstances than to start all over again from scratch.

The enemies around the Jews ensured they stayed captivated by their victim mentality; they sent threats and fear into their direction. They had better remember how emotionally, physically, and spiritually broken they still were and make no attempt at protest. The message was received loud and clear: to delay, to cling to the past, and to all the wrongdoings, *that* was by far the more familiar and safest option. They painfully swallowed the lie to accept their current circumstances.

In reality, the Jews' enemies feared the day they would unite and operate in full strength again. They were preventing their unity. The chosen people actually posed a threat to them. Over time, some of the Jews returned in groups to Jerusalem and started to rebuild the temple. After Zerubbabel, the governor of Judah, laid the foundation of the second temple, the construction of the rest of the temple came to a halt for another seventeen years (Ezra 4:24). Without the city walls to protect them, the Jews were vulnerable and exposed. They were also unable to progress with the rest of the temple's construction. No building could take place due to the lack of protection and proper resistance that city walls were meant to provide.

That was the case, until Nehemiah stepped to the front and decided to take on the rebuilding of Jerusalem's walls. He didn't accomplish this out of his own strength but with God's favour and provision (Nehemiah 2:8). Maybe it all seemed impossible to the Jews. Maybe they were just so depressed, tired, and ashamed of their past. Maybe they were even too scared to hope and believe that restoration was even possible?

Building is time-consuming, requires energy, strength, perseverance, and is very costly. It's a messy situation, a challenging process. It requires vision as well as the time and the will to follow through with it. Combine this challenging process with constant opposition from the outside, and who would want to get involved in such a hopeless scenario? Little did God's chosen people, His children, know how God would provide physically, emotionally, and financially in all of their needs during the restoration process. Little do God's chosen people, His children, still realise this truth today. The enemy probably has you caught up in the same type of lies at this very moment that also hindered and frustrated the chosen people in the past.

Even though human beings act contradictorily, God never changes. He is still the God that is, that was, and always will be. He's still the God that hears, sees, provides, and is actively involved in the restoration of His kingdom's broken walls. The enemy is all too eager to get us to passively stare at the brokenness within and around us.

Passive pain—the powerfully active yet passive lie that wants to come and steal our hope! That encourages us to stare, hands invisibly tied behind our backs, at the great and important work in front of us, around us, and inside of us!

God is almighty, and His Holy Spirit is powerfully active in the restoration of God's image on earth through the restoration of each person and the relationships among them. In some incredible and miraculous way God is busy leading us to reflect a shadow or pattern of His heavenly kingdom. We are already busy living out a truth of eternity. Since the fall, the whole of creation and every person craves the promise of restoration that God has already put into motion (Romans 8:20–21).

It's time to wipe the building dust from your eyes and to see that He, your loving heavenly Father and Creator, is hard at work within and around you.

God is already busy with your spiritual renovation!

It's time to truly realise that He has an unbelievable plan to make everything work together for your good and for His glory (Romans 8:28). It's time that you experience His love for you. It's time that you trust Him with this hectic, messy, yet breathtakingly beautiful space and time on earth that we know as life. It's time to find your hope again and anchor yourself to the timeless truth of your existence. It's time to broaden your vision because this process on earth is only the beginning. Amazing things await you after this life!

You have to hold on to this truth and remind yourself about it, especially on the days when the building process will feel unbearable and impossible. You have to cultivate an eternal kingdom-focused vision to persevere in this challenging building process on earth. There is *a reason* for your existence. There is *a plan*. What happens *now* really matters. *You* matter!

Jesus himself said that He came to give us life in abundance (John 10:10). What does that mean in a life full of physical, emotional, and spiritual pain? You may be asking yourself if you're missing or misinterpreting something. Why does the abundant life seem to avoid you and feel so unattainable?

Jesus has already started the renovation process at the cross and with the outpouring of the Holy Spirit at Pentecost (Acts 2). Actually, this restoration plan was already set in place at the very beginning (Genesis 3:15), where we were promised that Jesus would save us. Even at the very beginning of creation, God already had a much greater plan, the Christ Plan, as loving safety net in place. Every moment, the restorative building project progresses. God is the Master Architect, managing this project to the finest detail. Later on, we are going to look at the Building Team and how God is perfectly managing the restoration of your soul and spirit to the outmost detail.

We as human beings, accept the lie way too easily that things are sometimes just too damaged to ever be repaired. Our carnal nature gives up, tries something new, but doesn't like damaged goods. We'd much rather prefer to receive a perfectly comfortable house than ruins requiring full time and ongoing renovation for life! Our definition and expectation of repair gets blurry and complicated when we shift our focus away from the gospel, God's kingdom, and His eternal purposes. This happens when we seek perfection rather than process, and when we look at works or methods rather than grace.

Maybe we need to redefine repair. Everywhere you look at people—even Christian believers—you will see broken individuals, broken marriages, broken family relationships, broken connections between parents and their children, and broken relationships among fellow Christian believers. Everywhere you look there are broken connections between God and His free, redeemed, yet still broken children.

As Christian believers, we are free and have the true living God on our side to assist us in building His kingdom. Actually, it's more accurate to say that we have God on our side to assist *Him*. We have the opportunity to be part of this extraordinarily amazing restoration process. We are allowed and encouraged to pray and cry out to a loving Father who hears us—the same God that heard Nehemiah's desperate prayer and answered it (Nehemiah 1:11).

To become actively involved in your heavenly Father's plan, first requires faith. Then the hard part follows where we have to pick up our building equipment and learn to utilise it according to the Holy Spirit's instructions. There *will* be pain—no transformation is possible without it! Conscious decisions and efforts will be essential. But you will experience a liberating sense of freedom because you have received the gift of free will to choose to what extent you *want* to be part of this process!

So many people call out to God for restoration and repair, without getting involved in the situation themselves. Many people wait for doors to open that never open because the door handles are not even tried. Some people wait, and wait, and wait...

They become downcast and depressed, while the tools to make an opening are right next to them. It's Biblical that there are times to wait, to consult God in prayer, and to *not* act from your own strength (Psalm 27:14, Psalm 5:3, Zacharia 4:6). It's also Biblical that there comes a time to take action (James 1:23–25). Faith without actions isn't faith at all. Faith without works is dead (James 26). Prayer, wisdom, and discernment are essential as God directs each believer's steps in this waiting-acting-process.

Too many people, and this is said with so much love and grace, don't want to offend God by taking initiative with their actions. This is understandable. It's difficult for Christians to know when to wait, and when to act, since both are such important Biblical disciplines. Many Christians only wait, for they fear doing things against God's will, without realising that God has made us active participants in His plan. God found it very good to create man and woman in His image and for His glory (Genesis 1:26–27). God chose to give us free will, chose to become man Himself in Christ, and chose to send His Holy Spirit to live inside of us. God decided that life would revolve around relationships. It's very clear that God created human beings to be in voluntary relationship with Himself and other people—not to be forced or controlled. We choose to love, to act, or to remain passive. *Some passive moments of waiting may even be disobedient when God is expecting of us to move beyond our comfort zone and act according to His truth in the Bible.* Miracles still happen where God provides unbelievable breakthroughs, instant healings, and unexpected physical means. However, no person is passively involved in the process. To be able to witness or experience an instant or a long-term miracle, requires *awareness*. Awareness again, requires your *attention and reaction*.

To be part of the restoration of God's kingdom is a miracle on its own! It doesn't fit the recognised category of immediately visible miracles that instantly take your breath away. However, it remains the greatest miracle of your life! Nothing about it is normal or ordinary. That's why it requires faith and being tuned in.

When you're actively involved in the process, you'll know it. Things will change inside of you. You will experience spiritual growth and healing taking place, which aren't always easy to explain. Sometimes, change will happen instantly, and other times it might take longer because the wound lies so much deeper, requiring more extensive repair. At times, you'll look back on your life, and marvel at how all the pieces fell perfectly into place. You'll see a picture coming together that you couldn't have predicted, and may never want to change in hindsight. You'll look back and realise that it's true that God makes everything work together for good. You will! And you will experience it as nothing other than the most astonishing miracle of your life!

Wisdom, that is still currently applicable to the restoration of God's broken people and broken earthly kingdom, can be found in the books of Ezra and Nehemiah. Both books have a strong building theme throughout. Whether you were aware or unaware, now is the time to realise anew that God is calling every single one of His children to be a builder of His kingdom. A very clear theme is woven into God's Word, from Genesis to Revelation: God intervening to restore the brokenness of His children by restoring His kingdom.

There's a gap in the wall that only you can fill. Nobody can do it on your behalf. The whole building loses its proper function and greater purpose with all the unrepaired gaps in it. Paul didn't refer to the Christian believers as "the body of Christ" for no specific reason. Your life is serving a valuable purpose, not only for yourself, but for every person around you—especially for your fellow believers in Christ. Your brokenness therefore affects not only yourself, but everyone around you. There's a reason why you feel so dissatisfied and depressed when your brokenness causes you to isolate yourself—you were never created to function on your own. Each of us receive the gifts of the Holy Spirit and the natural abilities, talents, passions, and a unique personality to serve the entire body.

You might view yourself as insignificant, but the whole body of Christ can't function properly without your contribution. Your gap matters! We need you. We need you to build with us. Together our living stones support one another and is held together by Christ as head (1 Peter 2:5). As the Head, He directs our actions. That hole inside your heart that aches so terribly and hurts the people closest to you, requires serious attention. It's such an eye sore for a reason; God's grace makes it impossible to miss! The Holy Spirit will continue to direct your attention towards it. It's part of God's perfect restoration plan.

It's only when our relationship with God is restored, that our image-bearing capacity can be transformed and restored.

Our unique road to recovery and our testimony again helps someone else with their own image bearing restoration process. This chain reaction of restored parts functioning in unity, is how the body of Christ displays God's image and His kingdom on earth.

We'll never experience the fullness and magnitude of God's image through the body of Christ while we resist the restorative work of the Holy Spirit within and among us.

Each one of us is purchased by Christ's blood and free to choose to what extent we want to participate in His restoration process. God doesn't expect you to try and fix the brokenness of the entire world. You are responsible for what He has specifically entrusted into your own hands and pressed upon your own heart to attend to. There's a reason for your uniqueness.

Nehemiah didn't appoint a select few to carry the entire responsibility and burden of rebuilding Jerusalem's walls. Each person and each family repaired the broken part of the wall in front of their own homes, and in this process the entire wall was repaired as a whole (Nehemiah 3:28). In the same way, individuals and families can pursue the original ideal God intended for marriages, families, and relationships, and make their own contribution to the restoration of society, of God's kingdom, and the body of Christ on earth.

The temple that was rebuilt under the leadership of Zerubbabel (the governor) and Ezra (the priest), couldn't function properly until the city walls were repaired. It's important to take note of this, because in a similar way the church of today, the body of Christian believers, can't function efficiently and purposefully if the individuals and families of which it consists of lacks unity and wholeness.

It's vital to understand that the intention of this book is not to promote feelings of guilt or to portray standards and ideals that are impossible to achieve. We are all imperfect human beings that would have been lost and destroyed if it wasn't for God's saving grace. We all need saving and restoration: Jesus Christ. This book acknowledges that every family doesn't represent the ideal family of a mother and father with their own offspring. The brokenness in which we find ourselves today, involves divorce, death, and sin that have changed family dynamics drastically to include grandparents, carers, godparents, foster parents, and single parents. This book is for everyone because everyone in this world is currently battling with some form of brokenness—their own, as well as their loved ones'. Each person's wholeness is contributing in some way to the greater wholeness of all. Your spiritual restoration—your living stones—provide support and an important function to the living stones next to you that are also being built up together in Jesus Christ. Whether we want to face it or not, we are all in this together and can't accomplish anything on our own. We were never lovingly designed for loneliness and pain.

God's saving, and healing grace meets everyone exactly in the circumstances they find themselves in. Sometimes the things of the past can't be completely restored or rectified but we can choose how we're going to build onwards from this point forward.

God's grace and love fills every crack in every stone that is being built up again. And in this process, He is already making everything new. In this process, He is making everything work together for good, just like He promised—maybe even better than we could ever imagine! There will probably always be cracked scars but a scar testifies about damage that has been repaired to ensure an even stronger functioning purpose. Even after Jesus was raised from the dead, He still bore the crucifixion scars visibly on His palms as a sign of the new covenant God has made with us: forever redeemed and destined for an eternity in God's presence! The grace found in the gospel turns all scars into a beautiful masterpiece.

If Jesus, in His full perfection, kept the scars related to our imperfection, we, in our imperfection, never need to be ashamed of the scars that testify about His healing grace in our lives (John 20:27).

To the contrary, the honesty of your scars may inspire, motivate, and activate other broken people to follow their healing journey with Christ. In this way, your greatest memory of shame may contribute to someone else's greatest breakthrough!

It's not always possible to forget. To forget can be dangerous. You might forget the wisdom and knowledge gained in the process to prevent the repetition of negative choices. This book won't encourage you to forget. This book will motivate you to remember because it's only by remembering that can we build the future different from the past.

God is calling all His children to rebuild and restore with Him. God is moving hearts to restore His broken kingdom and the broken body of believers. God is calling *your* heart. He is busy with the spiritual renovation of individuals and families, where hearts are being turned to one another, so spiritual transformation and healing can take place within individuals and also within their relationships, circling out to the rest of the believers. This spiritual renovation has a true effect on the rest of society. God is calling the youth to build on the right foundation and to be witnesses for Christ. The Holy Spirit is restoring the discipleship of parenting and mentoring in the hearts of carers and role models. The Holy Spirit is also busy to accentuate the body of Christ as a whole—the needs, the functions, and what it means to love and serve.

You will never be able to grow or fully enjoy the fruit of the Holy Spirit while you are living in emotional isolation. You also won't get to taste and experience the fruit of the Holy Spirit in other believers. Their fruit was meant to be a precious gift to *you.*

You will experience joy on a whole new level, once you start to live out your divine purpose, by being your unique self, filled with the Holy Spirit, serving others with your natural and spiritual gifts. Being unique isn't a curse. It's a blessing—with a responsibility. Somehow the carnal world has influenced our minds to follow trends, to fit in, to do what is expected and accepted as the norm.

The blessing of each unique member only reaches its full effect once that member is embraced, celebrated, and encouraged to serve other members with their unique passion. Your enemy might try to convince you that you don't belong and have nothing to offer—this is only his deceptive way of keeping you from your calling and purpose within the body of Christ. Not only does he intend to hurt you by doing this, but also everyone around you. One of his greatest missions is to destroy unity. Remember how he used deception in the garden of Eden to break the unity between Adam, Eve, and God. By using deception, he presented twisted facts to Adam and Eve that made them doubt God's original instruction. He also activated their pride by convincing them that they could be like God if they ate the forbidden fruit. Not only did he succeed in breaking the unity in the relationship that God had with Adam and Eve, both separately and conjoinedly, but also between Adam and Eve—the first broken marriage in history. That was the moment pride and brokenness entered the world.

The enemy is still using deception and pride to withhold you from the restoration of unity between your spirit and God's Holy Spirit, and within your meaningful relationships. Love and relationship are concepts so deeply interwoven that it's impossible to define the one without the other. God is love (1 John 4:8). And God, who is Spirit (John 4:24) and is Christ (John 1:18), is relationship. It's difficult to get our human minds around this and requires acceptance through faith. You were created in His image—for love and for relationship—all for His glory. John goes as far as to say that those who do not love, do not know God, for God is love.

We not only serve a God of love and relationship, but a God of restoration and hope. Your brokenness is a blessing in disguise because restoration and hope displays God's love for you!

God never changes. His will for us never changes. We might not physically build His kingdom with stones and concrete and we know that God's presence doesn't require physical walls or structures to manifest (John 4:21). The good news Jesus brought us, proclaims that everyone who believes in Him, has access to our heavenly Father and that His presence now resides within us.

When Jesus died on the cross, our sins died with Him. The veil in the temple that blocked the access to the Holies of Holy, God's throne, was torn open. There's nothing that separates us from God. With God's Spirit inside of us, our relationship with God is restored. We receive the Holy Spirit as seal (2 Corinthians 1:21–22). Yes, we already receive eternal life in the Spirit, streams of living water, before we even die (John 7:38). We don't necessarily live in Jerusalem and the new Jerusalem will only be established with Christ's return, but what do we do in the meanwhile? What do we do while we're waiting for Christ's return and God's kingdom to be fully and eternally restored?

Jesus taught us to pray and ask that God's kingdom come and His will be done on earth, as it is in heaven. He also taught us to seek God's kingdom first and above all things (Matthew 6:10). The Holy Spirit within us guides and teaches us to pursue this to bring God's kingdom to earth.

Holy restoration is the heartbeat of the Holy Spirit!

This holy restoration process includes every human being's relationship with their heavenly Father, the restoration of relationships within marriages, families, communities, and the inner restoration of every individual. This is the restoration of God's kingdom on earth, little by little, until His kingdom will finally be restored forever with Christ's return. God is building us up, moment by moment, taking us from glory to glory, until the day that we'll be as glorious as Christ (2 Corinthians 3:18). Your righteousness is already restored in Christ. How do you build upon His righteousness throughout the rest of your living days?

Do you also hear the invitation deep within you to come and participate in the restoration of His broken walls?

Filling the Gap

I stand in awe as I struggle to comprehend:
The impact of my contribution to Your kingdom –
To what extent?
For I am so inferior and imperfect
Withdrawing from You and others
Avoiding possible pain –
My soul, I try to protect,
But in doing so, I was caught up in a lie
Causing even more pain—not only mine...
Isolation hurts!
It's not only I who thirsts
This weakness is contained and fed by my fears
Not only robbing the reaching of my God-given potential
But also trying to steal my heavenly credentials
It tries to destroy Your perfect plan
For me and all of man:
Community –
I never fully realised
Or owned my part and responsibility
In the optimal functioning of Your earthly body
I find new revelation in all that I am –
Yóúrs!
To share with óthers
And in this holy unity
I finally understand what it means to be
Happy...
Happiness is only real when shared
Communion equals broken shared bread
And restoring relationships restores Your image: Love
Within this unity I find what has been lost
And share it freely,
The greatest gift is in the giving:
All purpose perfected by serving
Amen.

Chapter 2

*And I will give you **a new heart**, and I will put a new spirit in you.
I will take out your stony, stubborn heart and give you a tender,
responsive heart. And I will put my Spirit in you so that you will
follow my **decrees** and be careful to obey my **regulations**.
—Ezekiel 36:26 (NLT)*

Something is starting to change. Something feels different. You
can't explain it precisely, and you don't know where it all is
heading. But you can definitely sense a change of direction. John
3:8 (NLT): "The wind blows wherever it pleases. You hear its sound,
but you cannot tell where it comes from or where it's going. So it
is with everyone born of the Spirit." You are experiencing *hope*.
You are ready for change and willing to do something about the
building rubble eyesore in front of you, within you, and around
you. There's just no way that you can or want to continue on like
before.

The first, biggest, and bravest step that you take, is to
look reality straight in the face. You acknowledge and confess
everything that has contributed to this big gap. From here on
forward, things will never exactly be the same as before. You don't
want to cover the gap up again with temporary solutions and false

structures. It doesn't make sense anymore, and it's time that you build your life properly to ensure *permanent sustainability.*

The shame of your brokenness and mistakes is handed over and dealt with. To your relief, your big gap is completely covered by *grace*—a real encounter with God's forgiveness and redeeming love. This grace-experience is so overwhelming! You might have heard a few things about it before, but you've never made it your own. You've never really received it before.

Cheap grace is an enemy—withholding us from true spiritual transformation. Cheap grace is deceptively entwined with the legalistic side of religion. Cheap grace uses guilt and required actions to make us acceptable to God, determining who qualifies to receive grace, and to what extent. It's only through faith and only by grace that we are redeemed and restored (Ephesians 2:8). It goes above and beyond all human reasoning how a just God can allow this, and yet He does. In Christ, justice was achieved. To accept Christ is to accept God's grace.

Before any construction can take place, the building site needs to be purchased and *legally owned.* Before any spiritual building can take place, it's essential to know who the owner of the site and process is.

Children of God need to understand and appreciate the truth that they belong to the only living God, the same God of Abraham, Isaac, and Jacob. He has called you by name and declared that you are His (Isaiah 43:1). Do you really believe it, and have you made it your identity? Do you know that you are incredibly loved and that you really belong to God?

Damaged property still legally belongs to the owner. The vandalization and destruction of God's property doesn't make Him less entitled to it. Even lost or stolen property still belongs to the original owner. The original building plan still belongs to God. The original design of God's kingdom still belongs to Him. The vision that God has for humanity and every single individual, still belongs to Him. God loves us so much that He purchased us back with Christ's blood (John 3:16), even though we were His from the very start. If anyone is unsure about to whom the kingdom really belongs, we have the proof in Christ! We live in exciting times where the mystery of the Christ Plan has been revealed to us.

It's very difficult to grasp God's love for humanity without understanding His grace and mercy. It's very difficult to love God without realising His love for you. We are able to love because He is love. The watering down of the gospel, leads to a very depressing and ugly image of the construction site.

Without a vision and without hope, this heap of building rubble would just look like a waste of time and effort. But combine it with an entrepreneur that has legal ownership, vision, unlimited resources, and suddenly the possibilities and future look completely different!

In the kingdom of God, renovation doesn't take place lightly. God completely rebuilds and restores, making all things new (Revelation 21:5). He builds new hearts, new spirits, and a new destiny. The wrong foundation simply won't do. Christianity isn't based on behavioural changes that lead to a change of heart, a change of heart is essential to lead to behavioural changes. The change takes place from the inside out, from the foundation upwards. The better the soil is prepared, the greater the harvest. The foundation determines the structure and the outcome.

The rebuilding of Jerusalem's walls started with a single outcry from the heart. Nehemiah asked his brother about the well-being of the Jews that had been released from captivity and that had returned to Jerusalem. We can apply this question today by asking about the well-being of the believers in Christ that have been released from the enemy and from sin's captivity—the free and redeemed children of God that are able to return to "Jerusalem". Those that are free to enter God's holy place and have direct access to His throne of mercy. Those that have the privilege to live in God's presence and be in relationship with Him through Christ.

Jerusalem has always been a very special and symbolic place. The temple that was built and rebuilt in Jerusalem is probably one of the most important buildings in history. We know that there has been a holy war over it for centuries! God gave very clear specifics on its design and construction. It also served more than one function. Not only did it serve as the place of worship that God had filled with His manifest presence, but it was also a shadow or visual presentation of God's heavenly temple and the way to access God's throne (Hebrews 8:5). By examining the design and details of the temple, we are given a glimpse of God's heavenly kingdom and His holiness. The temple was built and destroyed three times. It was never rebuilt after its destruction in 70 AD. Today we know that God manifests His presence inside of us. We are His temple (1 Corinthians 3:16). We, as believers, form the church. God continually manifests His presence in us by filling us with His Holy Spirit (Acts 13:52). God is busy building us up spiritually to dwell within and among us as His spiritual house (1 Peter 2:5).

The building process of today now focuses on the spiritual restoration of God's kingdom within every individual and relationship. When Jesus returns, the true temple and new Jerusalem will be forever restored—direct access to God like in the garden of Eden. No temple or place of worship will ever be needed again (Revelation 21:3). No symbolical descriptions, shadows, or patterns will be needed then. We, as Christian believers, have the privilege of waiting expectantly to see Jerusalem made new and entering eternal life with God.

But what happens in the meantime? Are we just going to look around at the broken temple and city walls of His kingdom on earth, while we wait for the heavenly one to be restored? Are we just going to passively wait for the better days of Christ's return while we sit among the building rubble of our own and others' lives? Is this the message that is found throughout the Bible?

There has to be a greater meaning, a reason, for our current existence. There has to be a reason why we have to finish this life on earth before we enter the eternal one. There has to be a reason why Jesus Christ came to earth, paid the price, ascended back to heaven, and sent us His Holy Spirit. There has to be a reason why God is allowing the here and now. The deep search for meaning within every soul reflects this truth—there's more to this current moment than what we can comprehend. There must be a reason why God has planted this search for meaning deep within every living heart and soul. There must be a reason why brokenness hurts as much as it does and why every human being long for restoration! We are definitely not being tortured and forced to live in brokenness, while a glorious spiritual restoration process is busy taking place!

Nehemiah refused to accept the Jew's brokenness. We have to realise that God doesn't let anything happen for no reason. He has a very special plan for every person's life. If you read the Bible from the front to the back and follow the storyline, you will pick up that there's a very specific plan playing out, and even repetitive patterns and messages that confirm one another. There's a reason why you were born, why you find yourself where you are right now, and where you are heading. A man plans his path, but the Lord directs his steps (Proverbs 16:9).

Jesus instructed His disciples to seek first the kingdom of God. It has to be a prayer request from the heart to experience God's kingdom on earth during our own lifetime. It's more than a request. It's a deep nestled longing for God's presence and holiness that we want to see and experience with our spirit. It really is an intense longing to be close to God again.

We are in so much pain when we live so far away from God and His original plan for humanity. Phillip Yancey explored the purpose and blessing of pain in his book *Where is God when it hurts?* Once we understand the incredible way the pain system functions, we come to realise what a gift and miracle it really is. Pain has an irreplaceable perfectly designed function. It's an indication that something within the body is wrong or in danger, and a warning signal that the body needs urgent attention for repair and healing to take place. In the same way emotional pain in our soul is an emergency signal for something that requires urgent attention, protection, and healing. *Only God can provide that type of emotional healing. All other temporary methods will fail.*

The beginning of this miracle of restoration starts when we are reborn of the spirit. We can't understand this with our natural mind and we won't be able to see it with our natural eyes. But God's Word promises that it is true (1 Peter 1:23). That is why we need to take that first step of the restoration process in faith. Don't harden your heart when you hear His voice (Hebrews 3:15). Even if the whole spiritual rebirth doesn't make sense to you, trust God. John 3:3 (NLT): Jesus replied, "I tell you the truth, unless you are born again, you cannot see the Kingdom of God." Jesus continues to explain in John 3:5–8 (NLT): "I assure you, no one can enter the Kingdom of God without being born of water and the Spirit. Humans can reproduce only human life, but the Holy Spirit gives birth to spiritual life. So don't be surprised when I say, 'You must be born again.' The wind blows wherever it wants. Just as you can hear the wind but can't tell where it comes from or where it is going, so you can't explain how people are born of the Spirit." So even though we can't explain this first part of our spiritual restoration, we can accept, and believe that it is really taking place. We will notice the effects and the fruit that is produced by it. We will notice a change in our invisible inner structure and outer visible actions.

Let's look at the Jews of Nehemiah's time from our current perspective, and find the truth of God's living Word that still reveals, guides, releases, and repairs. More than that, let's look again at God's entire story—one great love story from beginning to end. One filled with a mysterious, miraculous plan. One immense promise that has been predicted, fulfilled, and keeps on being fulfilled until it will reach its glorious final perfection.

Maybe it feels as uncomfortable to you as it did for me, to read about Jerusalem, Israel, and God's chosen people, as if it forms part of your own life and future, even when you're not part of the nation. There was a time I honestly felt a bit rejected and jealous about not being a direct descendant of the chosen Jewish people. It felt a bit unfair to be seen or described as a gentile without any say or choice in the matter, and made me feel far away from God's promises and plans in the Bible. When I first read the Bible from that angle, it actually felt a bit impersonal to me. It almost felt like I was reading a love letter addressed to someone else. However, the incredible truth is that, although God demonstrates His plan through His involvement with the chosen Jewish people, everything is applicable to every believer in Christ. It's only by understanding the entire history of the Bible, the history of the Jews, and God's intervention with the chosen people, that we get to understand our own salvation and the bigger picture. That is why we can't read certain parts of the Bible or only look at certain Bible verses. We have to read the entire Bible to understand the entire story.

We, as gentiles, are not rejected or excluded but totally included in this everlasting covenant with God. In Galatians 3:28 Paul, who was appointed by Christ to reach the gentiles, says that there are no longer Jews or gentiles, slave or free, man or woman, because we are all one in Jesus Christ. Of course, you are still a man or a woman and have a specific cultural background—Paul meant that none of these classifications determine who qualifies to receive salvation and eternal life and who not. Every person that accepts Jesus Christ as The Way to God, forms part of God's chosen and anointed children.

With this truth of inclusion in mind, look again at the Jews of Nehemiah's time—see them as the spiritual family you belong to now. They were free! They had free will. They could go and do whatever they wanted to do. Slavery and captivity just formed part of the bad memories of their past. But still, their past clung to them like old rags and shaped a big part of their identity, causing them to function like oppressed people. One has empathy for their reaction, as we are so aware of the fact that we also face the same challenges daily in many ways and various levels of intensity. Drifting around without a clear vision, without a dream. Feeling dejected and rejected. Being exposed without city walls to provide protection. Being free but living as if still in bondage—conditioned and bound to an illusion, a lie. Bound to a lie that Jerusalem will never be restored as before or that it'll never be as wonderful and glorious as in the beginning. Feeling vulnerable and noticing the broken walls that needed mending yet staying passive and powerless. Does it feel familiar?

Nehemiah's reaction was far from passive! His heart was completely shattered! He cried, fasted, and prayed. He entered a deep phase of mourning, so upset that he was unable to eat, so desperate for God to hear his outcry, praying for his people day and night (Nehemiah 1:4).

God's heart resonated with Nehemiah's request. Jesus said that when we first seek the kingdom of God, the rest will also be given (Matthew 6:33). Maybe seeking God's kingdom is everything we need. Nehemiah seeked God's kingdom and had a burning passion for the restoration of God's kingdom and His chosen people. God must have been satisfied with this request, for He answered the prayer and His favor rested on Nehemiah. This gives us a glimpse of what it means to seek God's kingdom first. It also provides us with a glimpse of God's will, plan, love, goodness, and glory. It displays God's heart for the restoration of His people—His heart for *your restoration!*

An indescribable thing happens when God's will and our heart's desires line up—miracles happen! Throughout the book of Nehemiah, we read about God's favor being with Nehemiah as He helped him to rebuild the city walls. This favor meant that God stepped in to make everything work together to accomplish this request and purpose. You, precious child of God, are also anointed with God's favor to accomplish His kingdom purposes in your life (1 John 2:27).

God never changes. He is still willing and eager to help us restore His kingdom. We're living in the last days, and we don't know how much time we have left before all the prophesies in Revelation are fulfilled. We also don't know how many days we have left in our temporary lives. The end of our lives, are in reality also our own end times, which could take place at any given moment. This means that we need to respond with even more urgency to this invitation of restoration!

The Christian faith is very unique, revolving around undeserved grace—the reason for the cross. Where some religions require works to obtain mercy and forgiveness, payment to receive righteousness, rituals to increase faith, and good deeds to enter positive eternal outcomes, the Christian faith accepts that nothing could ever be done by our own human efforts to make us right with God. Christians—disciples of Jesus Christ—believe that everyone, even the best and most disciplined person, is sinful due to the fall and that we can't do anything to save or sanctify ourselves. The sacrificial cleansing of the Old Testament was only a shadow of the true sacrifice that would come—Jesus Christ, the Lamb without blemish (John 1:29). Instead of feeling dejected by the fact that there's nothing we could do on our own to make us right with God, we should celebrate and rejoice with overflowing gratitude! God already did all the hard work! He took it on Himself and we only need to join the process!

A change of heart, a confession, a genuine need for God's grace, is only possible when you really look at the condition of your soul and see it as it truly is. Without that awareness of your sin, salvation, restoration, and healing are impossible outcomes. A change of heart is also essential to start the repair of broken relationships in our marriages and families. That's why it's not a bad thing at all to hit rock bottom—uncomfortable and painful for sure, but desperateness and urgency are powerful hidden blessings that bring our world to a standstill, and awaken what God has originally planted in our being.

Emotional pain is an emergency signal launched from the soul to be seen and heard. This signal won't stop the alarm if you cover your spiritual ears. Like the park distance control function of a vehicle, the signal is only going to escalate into a faster and louder mode as you move closer to the danger zone. The best thing, and actually the only thing you could do, would be to stop, look around you and change the direction you were moving in. The first step into His healing light, is to be honest with yourself and to acknowledge that something isn't right. It's like a GPS that keeps on rerouting, continuously encouraging you to make a U-turn. It's a voice you can't turn off when you're driving on the wrong route and heading in the wrong direction.

Physical pain often involves inflammation—the body's natural reaction when tissue gets damaged. Although the inflammation is painful and hinders normal physical functioning, it serves a vital function—it covers and protects the tissue that got damaged and provides the right condition for healing to take place with as little interference as possible. Any action that could cause further and permanent damage triggers a painful response.[1] The inflammation brings everything to a halt and calls for steady support, some seclusion, and even rest.

Stillness. Awareness. Adjustment. Healing.

Every member within the whole body of believers, is supposed to get affected by the pain of another member. We must be aware of the attention and care that need to be provided to hurting members. Our individual and combined awareness should reach beyond ourselves. No pain should ever be dealt with all alone. We are to carry each other's burdens (Galatians 6:2). You are allowed to send out pain signals—loud and clear for the rest to hear. You are supposed to share your doubts and troubles with

---

[1] *Yancey, P. Where is God when it hurts? p.35*

another compassionate person. Your neighbour is also allowed this privilege.

Pain isn't supposed to be suppressed or hidden. The inflammation reaches beyond the wounded area, alerting the cells around it of the presenting situation. Depression and anxiety are taking over control within the body of Christ because its members have decided to suppress and deny the presence of pain, damage, emotional, and spiritual brokenness. We are all confused and scared to be vulnerable, because some of the members within body of Christ have forgotten how to respond appropriately, or simply refuses to respond to the need right in front of them. We've all been hurt in some way by the very members that form part of our spiritual body. The Holy Spirit that we share, have been hurt by these actions. So, we choose to hide our true emotions and suppress our desperate need for support and connection! We isolate ourselves, doubt our feelings and get stuck in this downwards spiral of a festering wound that we're sitting in. The wound won't be able to heal due to a lack of knowledge, compassion, grace, and love. You won't be able to heal in isolation. That person you are so aware of, that is stuck in a destructive pattern, won't be able to heal if no-one reaches out to them.

Instead of healthy cells, working together to combat the spiritual diseases taking over our united body, some of us have become cancer cells—taking up space, multiplying pointless outcomes, only focusing on our own advancement and needs, and slowly suffocating the life of the Holy Spirit out of the cells that are so desperate in need of Him!

Physical and emotional pain both play very powerful and important roles within the body of believers. A broken heart is one that aches with spiritual inflammation, and just like physical inflammation, it begs to be still, to receive firm support, to be held in a safe place, and to rest. We need to provide that environment of rest and support to our aching members. We also need to encourage these members to rest in God's presence.

We'll never be able to fulfil all of God's work through the body of Christ. We are privileged to be part of it, and God uses our willingness to touch other people. But He is a jealous God (Exodus 34:14), wanting a direct relationship with each of His children. There are things that can only be restored by His Word, His revelatory truth, and personal prayers in relationship with Him. We might cringe at the idea that God is "jealous". That might be the case because we have experienced all the ugly effects of human jealousy. This jealousy is actually beautiful when it's put into the right context—God is yearning to guard what is His, to protect and keep us safe from the evil one, to cherish the apple of His eye. He doesn't want us to get lost in meaningless relationships with worldly, harmful idols.

God calls His children to be still, to know that He is God, to turn back to Him, to repent of the damages done, to hand over the battle, and to receive the healing that only He is able to offer. He invites and encourages you to enter His rest. It's within this rest, within this stillness, knowing, waiting, and trusting, that emotional and spiritual healing can take place. In Chapter 8 we look at God's rest and what it really means for the Christian believer of today.

God is more than able and more than willing to repair and restore what you hand over to Him. Let's not limit God or place Him into boxes. He can and will do even more than that, but He seems to be working with us through our faith in Him and our relationship with Him. He calls us, leads us, and intervenes, but He never ignores or suppresses our free will. No- one wants to be in a relationship where they are forced to love. Forced love could never be real love. Every person is born with the vital need to give and receive unconditional love. Without it, no one would be able to survive. Love is part of our original design—the very fingerprints of God that stayed behind when He created us.

Every honest person will admit that bought love, could never fill up their love tanks. Love that needs to be bought or forced, requires constant control and manipulation. There's no truth in manipulation. According to Genesis, we were made in God's image. We can't talk on God's behalf, but one may wonder that if God created us with this strong need for unconditional love, how much greater is God's will that His image-bearers seek Him out of love and just love Him for Who He is?

We think we know what love is. We experience some of it and try to verbalise it. We struggle to get away from it and we long for more of it. Only the Creator of love can teach and guide you in the truth of love.

Only the Creator of love can show you its function and power. Only the Creator of love can increase the love in your heart and bring it to life. You will never experience true love apart from God.

Like a good, good Father, better than any earthly imperfect father, God draws you closer to Him, to willingly hand over your brokenness to Him. God invites you, through Christ, to hand over the rubble of your life for Him to repair and restore in relationship with Him. There is healing in His unconditional love. Trust Him to take your brokenness, your mess, and to transform it into a masterpiece! He knows exactly what you need. Matthew 7:11 (TPT) "If you, imperfect as you are, know how to lovingly take care of your children and give them what's best, how much readier is your heavenly Father to give wonderful gifts to those who ask Him?".

God is able and God is busy to rebuild His broken children. He is busy healing and repairing from the foundation upwards. Individuals, marriages, families, and relationships are being rebuilt and restored by His Spirit. He lays His foundation as soon as the soil of your heart is exposed, cleared, and prepared. It's only when our own broken relationship with God is restored, that our relationship with ourselves and others can also be restored. What you put in, you will get out. You will harvest what you plant

(Galatians 6:7). *Broken people using their own strength to battle other broken people, just create more brokenness.*

A change of heart will always involve the laying down of one thing, in order to receive the other. Pride will be replaced by humility, and don't we all know how brokenness can break our pride! Contrary to what we believe, this is a special place to be because pieces of lies are also being broken off, exposing truth. What is true in the light, has always been true in the dark. Knowing and acknowledging the truth, will set you free. It's spiritually painful to stay seated in the dark with the truth right there with you all the time but refusing to allow the light to enter.

Trying to repair broken pride with some more pride, is like building a tower with blocks that aren't aligned, convincing yourself that the blocks won't fall. The darkness steals your vision, your peace, your time, and finally your life. It truly is the biggest tragedy, because it needn't be that way. The enemy only came to kill, steal and destroy (John 10:10). He is the father of lies (John 8:44). Jesus Christ came so that we could live in the light, know the truth and be free. If you have Jesus, you have life. Whoever doesn't have the Son of God, doesn't have life (1 John 5:12). And if the Son sets you free, you will be free indeed (John 8:36). By handing over your rubble mess willingly, God can clear the site of your heart and build on His intended foundation—for your life, and His kingdom. You were created first and foremost by God, for God, and your restoration will need to start at the original purpose. From then on forward, God can and will build on your life and relationships because it brings His kingdom to earth. It brings Him much joy and glory when we build our lives aligned with His truth—straight and strong structures, able to provide resistance during the storms of life.

A change of heart is so easy, yet so difficult. So complicated but in reality, so simple. It all starts with a heart that says sorry. We confess our sins to God, moving our hearts in line with His grace, placing ourselves humbly and dependant under His loving maintenance. We can enter His presence and let go of our shame. God already knows everything—whether we confess it or not. The confession then, has little to do with exposing what is already known to God but a lot to do with a change of heart and what is known to us. We decide to move away from our own control, determination, and the lie that we're able to fix our own and other people's brokenness on our own.

We also need to say sorry to the people in our lives that form part of our moulding process. Blessed are the peace makers, for they will be called children of God (Matthew 5:9). Sometimes you even need to forgive yourself—for what you've done or have neglected to do, for what you have allowed or have resisted. Just like David, we can ask God to search our hearts and show us what needs attention (Psalm 139:23). If every single one of us are imperfect, then it's impossible that some of us will be able to do everything right the whole time. Consciously and subconsciously, we hurt other people, push them away, isolate ourselves, fight back with self-justification, or try to force our own will on others. The less control we hand over to God, the harder we'll try to control everything ourselves. If you look closely at a conflict situation, you'll see that the trouble entered by the way we tried to take complete control of a situation or another person. In stead of allowing God to shape us and loving shaping one another, we end up chiselling away at each other, encouraging more pride than change of hearts.

In this broken, fallen world, all of us have gotten hurt. Certainly, there isn't even one person that could say that they have only experienced perfect happiness without any pain. Not even Jesus, who never sinned, was spared from heartbreak. What an astonishing and liberating truth to know that God doesn't reject us because of our brokenness but chose to become equal in our brokenness in Jesus Christ in order to overcome it!

Many of us have shut our hearts in an effort to avoid more heart ache. The sad truth is that the wound within can't be dealt with and can never get healed. It can't just disappear. It's also impossible to hand out something that you haven't first received. It's impossible to receive grace if your heart is closed off, and thus impossible to share grace with those in dire need of receiving it.

In order to rebuild the entire wall, some walls that were built to keep others out, need to be broken down first. We need healthy boundaries but we also need connection and relationship. Therefore, we need walls with gates. The Boundaries book series by Dr. Cloud and Dr. Townsend, excellently explain how we can build our walls according to Biblical truths, maintaining functional boundaries yet not living isolated or closed off. We want to keep the enemy outside and not become our own greatest enemy or an enemy to those who need us.

What seems impossible with humans, is possible with God! He said Himself that He will take out our hearts of stone and give us a new spirit, and a heart of flesh. He promises throughout the books of Jeremiah and Isaiah to restore the broken ruins—to restore *you*!

This restoration process is part of discipleship, which we'll be exploring in Chapter 5. In short, a disciple is someone that follows their teacher's ever move, deed, belief—literally living out their example. A disciple bears the image of their teacher by living exactly in the same way. We are in Christ, Christ is in us.

When Jesus invited His chosen disciples to follow Him, He believed in their ability to follow His example and live out His teachings. They were just normal, average, weak, and broken people like we are. When He commanded His disciples to go out to the corners of the earth and make people His disciples, He believed in the rest of humanity's ability to be His disciples as well. That means Jesus believes in *your* ability to live out His teaching and display His example.

This has nothing to do with legalistic expectations but everything to do with your image-bearing restoration.

The process through which God rebuilds and restores your

life on the Cornerstone, Jesus Christ, is part of the discipleship process. The first step in becoming a disciple of Jesus, was to follow Him. It's an invitation that requires a change of heart, a whole change of direction. It requires leaving your old life behind in order to follow His direction for your life. As we follow Jesus, we are systematically rebuilt and restored in His image.

With this choice to leave behind our old lives, we also leave the brokenness and mess behind that formed part of it. This is where we accept Jesus Christ and receive salvation—our eternal restoration. God believes in your restoration! Jesus keeps on transforming you into His original plan and into His image. The Holy Spirit moves with this process and guides your every step. Sometimes you'll only understand when you get to look back. Sometimes you're unaware of what He is busy changing within you, and other times the revelation in your heart is intense and clear. It's a process only you can partake in with the Lord and not everyone will always understand the details involved. It's a process you can't predict or control, but one that you can approach with hope and an expectant heart. And lots of trust—God is in control of the building process. Psalm 127:1 (NLT) "Unless the Lord builds a house, the work of the builders is wasted. Unless the Lord protects a city, guarding it with sentries will do no good."

Even though this is a path that only you can walk with God, you needn't do it in painful isolation. Other believers are there to encourage you and stand beside you. Other believers are there to protect you from deception, spiritual infection, and to provide an environment for healing and rest to take place.

We easily forget that other believers are also broken people busy in their own restorative process-journey with God. We forget that everyone is vulnerable and exposed. Too often we place so much pressure and form such high expectations of other believers to help us along in our restoration building process, while we remain a bit passive. As members of Christ's body, we need to extend more grace, knowing we're all facing similar challenges in this life. At times some believers are stronger and in better positions to help the weaker members. No-one is immune to the hardships of life and there will be days when the stronger members also experience weakness or temptations. We all need each other. No matter how hard we try to hide our weaknesses or how great we look on the outside, or on social media, be assured—we are all broken in various ways.

Restoring Heart Foundations

I give the pieces of my broken life, heart and soul
To You, oh living God, to make it whole
You are the only true Restorer
The Way and my safe border
The Rock and original Foundation
Since the beginning of creation
Restore Your holy temple now
In my humble need I bow
Your kingdom come
And will be done
Make me a living stone
Placed close to Your throne
Place me in line with Your Cornerstone
And breath over my spiritually dead bones
Abba Father,
Restore Your heavenly and earthly homes.
Amen.

Chapter 3

The Building Team (God): God as Architect, Jesus as the Building Plan, Holy Spirit as Builder

His eyes of faith were set on the city with unshakable
*foundations, whose **architect and builder** is **God** himself.*
—Hebrew 11:10 (TPT)

You realise that you can't manage this whole transformation process on your own. You ask yourself how you ever believed that you could. Some days you get distracted. You forget and try to pack a stone here and there on your own, only to experience disappointment and frustration as you chisel it out again, and wait for the right guidance. You admit that you lack the right knowledge and that your vision can become limited and distorted. You don't want to try and do it on your own anymore. Why would anyone try to do something so complicated on their own, if the best company and helper is available? There's an ongoing battle between your consciousness and subconsciousness that you can't control, and your faith in your own abilities is shaky.

With your heart being open and prepared, you sense a new dependence in your being. A radical shift has taken place, a humble submission. The guilt and burdens have been handed over with this shift. All the broken places are exposed and instead of experiencing the rejection you have anticipated, grace and healing approach you. From now on, you want to build carefully, the right way.

It's here, heart exposed, that you are ready to get to know your Building Team. It's here, that you get to sit in on the greatest meetings of your life! Here, you get to receive and exchange the most amazing ideas within a safe relationship with your Building Team.

It's at this stage of development, that you start to understand something about God's strategy and design for humanity and for yourself. Here, that your journey starts in understanding how your unique features form part of it all. You're not only going to listen to the panel, though there will be times when you'll be quiet. You'll be listening *and* processing. But you're also going to share your heart and thoughts. You're going to accept and agree, but you are also, honestly and realistically, going to question the design and purposes of the details at some stages. You have received the freedom to do this from your Building Team. Yes, it's allowed. The Psalms testify about your freedom to share all your emotions, thoughts, and longings. God called David a man after His own heart (Acts 13:22). Your voluntary contribution is a thing of beauty and great joy to your Building Team. They actually delight in your participation! Without your input, the construction can't take place. "Do not despise these small beginnings, for the Lord rejoices to see the work begin, to see the plumb line in Zerubbabel's hand." (Zechariah 4:10, NLT).

You are safe here. You are loved. Beloved. Be loved.

Your Building Team wants to inform you, but also wants to receive your own input. They also ask for your trust in the areas where your understanding is insufficient. Sometimes you don't understand the reason or the process, but you are beginning to learn to trust and be patient. There are days you wish that the building process could speed up; days that you want to see the end in sight. But you're also learning that everything cannot and does not need to take place at your speed, on your timing, or according to your conditions.

The main purpose in life is to construct a building that will last forever. This requires a vision for the eternal future and the laying down of many temporary ideas.

It isn't always easy to stay focused. There are times that you feel frustrated and ungrateful for the Building Team's plan and process. There are times that you feel tired and fed-up, ready to grab hold of the next best alternative solution. Fortunately, you have a very stable and reliable Building Team that doesn't change course. You were informed of this the day you signed the contract. Maybe you signed before reading all the fine print, but you are busy processing all the information and truth. You are busy learning and busy moving your vision for the building structure in line with your Building Team's vision.

When you look back one day, after the final touches have been added to your building, you will have no words to express your appreciation and amazement. Everything—every single detail—will come together perfectly, making sense and being utterly functional. There will be no regrets that you've chosen this Building Team, who actually chose you first.

God as Architect of our lives

When we look at God as the Architect of the universe, Who lay the foundation of the earth (Job 38:4–5) and orchestrates every detail of our lives (Jeremiah 1:5), there are no words our human minds can produce to fully understand and describe Him or give Him enough honour and glory. Often, we speak so easily of God, with God and even *for* God. According to Isaiah 55:8 God's ways are higher than ours and His thoughts are not the same as our thoughts.

Humbly, with respect and admiration, we need to be careful not to unconsciously limit God or share His ways according to our own standards and perspectives. We need to fear Him out of love—a good type of fear that acknowledges Him as the holy and almighty King of the universe. Without realising it, we may ironically and with the best intentions, try to fulfil God's role ourselves. Being so misled by our own pride and agenda, we use God to justify our own messages and actions, without even first seeking Him in prayer and seeking His Word.

It's my sincere prayer that the content of this book honours God and builds His kingdom, without adding or taking anything away from His revelation truth in the Bible. Galatians 6:1-10 encourages each one of us to make a proper study of our own work, not comparing or thinking too high of ourselves. We each must carry our own load. Galatians 6:4–5 (MSG): "Make a careful exploration of who you are and the work you have been given, and then sink yourself into that. Don't be impressed with yourself. Don't compare yourself with others. Each of you must take responsibility for doing the creative best you can with your own life."

Each member of the body has a special function and purpose. Although we help carry each other's burdens, we need to carry our own load. A burden is a load too heavy to carry. But we have each received our own unique load to carry, one that God promises won't be too heavy and for which He provides enough strength. You may call this load your purpose or your calling. It's what you have received to carry and to work with during your time on earth. We don't compare our loads with one another. We trust that God knew exactly what He was doing when He put every detail of our lives together for His purposes. Don't become wary with comparison and envy. Your own load has everything you need to fulfil your own purpose. By trying to take on someone else's load, you are actually starting to carry a burden because that load was never yours to carry and it will also never feel comfortable. Make a careful exploration of who you are, what you have been given in your own load to carry, and be creative in utilising it to the best of your abilities—glorifying God the best way you possibly can.

This is the reason why this book was written. Prayerfully studying God's Word and doing proper introspection, has led to a deeper understanding of who I am and the gifts God has entrusted me with. I unpacked my load and carefully studied what I've been carrying since I can remember. He has given me a burning passion for words, books, reading, and studying. To do research and analyse everything that comes to mind, feels like second nature to me. My soul has ached for many years, as it felt like I was living without a passion and not fulfilling my purpose. I've come to realise that I'm not the only who experience this discomfort—this type of void and depression. I believe there's a very important reason why we experience this intense discontent and dissatisfaction deep within ourselves.

It's as though God has created a unique architectural drawing inside of our core that keeps on guiding us back to our original design—His unique plan and purpose for our existence. For this book's purpose: *a unique building plan.* A building plan that forms part of a much greater Building Plan. Without your part, the building plan is incomplete and without the complete building plan your part is isolated and meaningless.

It's impossible to find your true identity and live out your true purpose without God, outside of the body of Christ. John 1:1 Jesus is called "the Word" that was with God since the whole beginning, became flesh and is at the same time also fully God. According to the footnote in The Passion Translation, the original Greek word "Logos" was translated to "Word" in the other Bible translations, but it can also be translated to "Message" or "Blueprint". [2]

Jesus, God in the flesh, the very expression of God, became the Message and became our Blueprint! There's no other building plan

---

[2] John: Eternal Love, The Passion Translation © p.11.

for your life! No other way—Jesus is The Way and Jesus is YOUR Blueprint. Jesus is your Building Plan!

It's as if the Holy Spirit within us, highlights our unique function in the body of Christ and guides us to live out our purpose. That's why your purpose will be lived out by serving and can never be attained in isolation. It's impossible. A purpose that only benefits yourself, can never be a true calling. We get to know ourselves as we get to know God. The Architect of your life has a very specific plan.

This book is an example of doing my creative best to glorify God and serve the members of the body of Christ. Stepping out in faith with what I have to offer, without any agenda and unaware of the outcome, I feel content. It's as though God has prepared me and filled my heart and mind with these words throughout my entire life—to share it. To make my contribution. And within this raw honesty, true to my whole being, I sense that I honour Him in the best way I possibly can. I think this might be the way it feels for everyone moving a little closer or deeper into their purpose—it feels right, it feels free, it makes sense, and it's possible to accomplish. Suddenly the load makes sense. Suddenly the load is useful and even interesting. It's not necessarily easy, but it's more comfortable to pursue than goals that don't align with your abilities or passions. It's liberating and leads to an indescribable type of joy to be yourself—to be the best version of yourself, for God, and for other people.

It's not selfish or a negative desire to want to be of value, to mean something, and to feel that you're fulfilling your function on earth. There's nothing wrong to desire living out your unique calling. It's part of God's perfect plan, for you and every human being, to belong and to make a valuable contribution to people's lives (Romans 12:5). If it weren't for this desire, community and relationships would be impossible.

This desire focuses your attention on the gap in the building that only you can fill.

To live unsatisfied and without a purpose, doesn't only affect yourself in a negative way, it affects all in a negative way! Each one of us misses out on a part of God's glory and His greater vision inside this emptiness that were meant to be filled with the gifts He has distributed among us.

It's easy to notice someone who flourishes in their calling. Their building plan just shines out of their whole being and has a tremendous positive impact on the people around them! Not only are they successful in what they pursue, but they are truly happy and thankful to be able to do what they love. Even though they work hard, disciplined in their actions, and have to make many sacrifices, their building plan makes sense to them. And with God in control, they bring life to God's design and stir people's hearts. By living out their building plan they inspire others to find their true building plans, to accept it, and even enjoy it! They are busy filling their gaps in the wall, providing support to the living stones that want to build with them and next to them. They are busy fulfilling their function in the body of Christ, benefitting all those around them. It's easy to be jealous of them—which in reality is a sign that you haven't yet found your place to unpack your load and flourish with it. I want to challenge you to view this from a positive perspective and to acknowledge the hunger in your soul to find your place to serve. I also want to challenge you to share in their joy, because in reality, it's actually part of your own joy! You get to build your living stones next to them and with them.

Maybe you feel like your life is too complicated and that you don't have the same opportunities or resources as they do. I want to challenge you once again to look at your gap in the wall from a different angle. Your purpose in life goes way deeper than your job description. The good news is that your spiritual and physical gifts are not attached to, or limited to your qualification or work environment. Some changes might be necessary for you to flourish optimally. But the biggest change required, is your trust in God to mould you and use you in every season of your life. Obedience to

His voice deep inside of you, will help you to move in line with His purpose for your life. The moulding we receive in uncomfortable seasons and places are valuable. It challenges us to change our questions and thoughts. Instead of asking which environment suits us the best, we might need to ask in which environment we can serve the best.

Begin with what you have.

God will guide and help you to find meaning in your life and to fulfil your purpose. By seeking His face, you have already fulfilled your main calling in life—to love God with all your heart, all your soul, and with your entire mind (Matthew 22:37). To accept Christ's salvation is the most important thing you could ever do.

This actually takes away a lot of pressure. To journey with God in a relationship is a great bonus and blessing. To live out your purpose won't necessarily only lead to comfort or joy. To lay down your life for the life that Christ plans for you, will always require sacrifices (Matthew 16:24). But you'll live a more fulfilling life throughout the process and make an everlasting impact.

I want to encourage you to make a proper, prayerful study of who you are. Take a good look at the load you have been give—the positive, and even the negative. God uses our weaknesses for His glory! Accept and appreciate your uniqueness.

Keep making appointments with your Architect, so you can understand His plan, and bring it to life. Think of a bird. It flies, builds nests, sings, and just brings glory to God by demonstrating what it was created to be and to do. Nature has unlimited awesome examples of animals and plants displaying God's glory, intelligence, and power without saying a word.

In the same way, each one of us brings glory and honour to God by just being who we are and doing what we were created to do. Although you're fulfilling your purpose on earth by means of an earthly body, never lose focus of God's eternal kingdom. Corinthians 5 explains how our bodies are only temporary dwelling places. Our heavenly dwelling awaits. Pursue the fulfilment of your unique function on earth with an eternal focus, helping others to be built up spiritually as well. Nothing on earth happens for no reason. Corinthians 5 also mentions that we'll be judged according to our deeds. Everything we do on earth, matters in eternity.

If we were created in God's image (Genesis 1:27), then each one of us represents something of God. From the most outspoken extrovert, to the most observant introvert, from the most adventurous achiever, to the most peaceful dreamer—each one of us were made in His image, and together we represent a much greater image than we could in isolation. Your unique design and everything pure that excites your heart, glorifies God, and reflects something of God as Designer and Architect to everyone you come into contact with.

How amazing that God wants to be in relationship with us. How astonishing that He shares His Building Plan with us and wants us to partake in the process! How much faith He has in us to show His image and heart to other people! How awesome that Christ doesn't leave us in the dark but gives us His Spirit, His light, to help us with His plan (John 14:26).

He is not just our heavenly Father, but the King of the universe and beyond, the Creator of every visible and invisible particle, the Ruler of the spiritual world and Lord of the heavenly armies (Psalm 46:7). The Bible stays the most accurate and purest source of information for anyone that wants to know God, and the Holy Spirit guides us to understand His Word. His word is alive, active, and powerful, sharper than any double-edged sword that penetrates between soul and spirit, and it tests every thought of the heart (Hebrews 4:12). Books—even ones like this one—help us to grow spiritually, but the Bible is irreplaceable!

In Hebrews 8:5 we read about the shadows or copies that point to heavenly realities. If many things on earth are only shadows of the greater spiritual reality, one may wonder what other things currently in today's world—and in your own life—serve as mere shadows of a greater reality. One can only wonder what the shadow patterns of your building plan are representing at the moment. The tabernacle served as a shadow or pattern of God's holiness and throne in heaven (Hebrews 8:5). The Passover lamb that was a physical, symbolic sacrifice, represented Christ— our true sacrifice for our sins (1 Peter 1:19). The role of the priest was a shadow of Jesus' role as our mediator between God and us (Hebrews 4:14). God even uses marriage as a symbol or shadow, pointing to Christ as our bridegroom that is coming to fetch us, His bride (Revelations 19:7).

At the same time, God is our Architect and our Heavenly Father. Just as in a loving parent-child relationship on earth, it looks like God has revealed some heavenly truths to us once again, a shadow of His relationship with you, His child. If we want to understand something about God's father heart for us, we can look at the relationship between parents and their children. This provides only a very limited understanding, seeing that God is perfect and we are imperfect. But it's still meaningful to explore. In a healthy parent-child relationship, unconditional love is the main element that stand out. Parents see their children's weaknesses and sinful nature but can't help to love them and appreciate their unique personalities. Parents are so aware of all the potential within their children that is just waiting to develop. They look at their children's natural abilities, spiritual gifts, and talents with so much joy, seeing how it enhances life, and make the whole world look like a much better place. Is this maybe how God as Father looks at us?

Parents that are tuned into their children's needs, know exactly when to encourage them, when to reward and praise them, when to withhold something, when and how to provide discipline, and also when and how to provide comfort. As children of God we experience all of this in relationship with Him. Sometimes it stands out clearly and sometimes we are completely unaware of the parenting role God is playing in our lives at a specific time.

God uses people, members of Christ's body, encouragement, Scripture, opportunities, and circumstances to motivate us into action—to experience blessings and good seasons where we see and taste the promised fruit. We also experience times when God feels far away, when it's difficult to hear His voice or feel His love, times we have to hold on to our faith and push through. The Bible even says God disciplines His children because He loves them (Hebrews 12:7). He never leaves us. He is always involved.

A parent's or caregiver's strong desire to give their best to develop their children's character, might also be a revelation of God's father heart for us. One of the toughest things some parents have to face is a child battling with brokenness, while knowing their child's wonderful potential and capabilities.

On the other side of the relationship, some parents fail their children by not being aware of their potential and breaking them down instead of building them up. This causes a very distorted shadow of what the parent-child relationship was supposed to be like. Some children that are part of a very dysfunctional family might struggle to grasp the beauty of this shadow and struggle to understand God's love for them. They might also struggle to view God as a father figure.

Jesus came to restore that image of God as our true heavenly Father. Everything He did and said, came directly from the Father. If you're battling to see God as your Father, spend time getting to know Jesus. As you start to see how Jesus, our Blueprint, fits into God the Father, and how your own blueprint fits into Jesus, your relationship with your heavenly Father will be restored.

As mentioned in the previous chapter, God, the Architect of the entire universe and your life, believes in your restoration and wants to rebuild you completely. He wants to make you new. His plan and His will are set. Every promise and prophecy in the Bible were fulfilled. He kept His covenant with His people. He was faithful in providing every blessing He promised and also faithful in providing the consequences of His warnings about judgement. *He will be faithful to you too.*

Jesus as the Building Plan:

Although it's very difficult for us to understand God's image, He has provided a means to assist and enhance our understanding—His image in Jesus Christ. Jesus Christ, Who was sent to earth, fully human yet fully God, to forever restore you for His glory. Colossians 1:15 states that Jesus is the image of the invisible God, the Firstborn of the entire creation. Hebrews 1:3 (NIV): "The Son is the radiance of God's glory and the exact representation of his being, sustaining all things by his powerful word. After he had provided purification for sins, he sat down at the right hand of the Majesty in heaven." Jesus Christ is the only name through which we can be saved (Acts 4:12). There's no other way to build your life.

The same glory that God has revealed through Jesus Christ, is also given to us. Romans 8:29–30 (NIV) explains that God *predestined* for us to be *conformed to the image of Jesus*, so that Jesus might be the *firstborn* among many brothers and sisters. *We* are those brothers and sisters. And because He has chosen us, He has also called us to Him. And because He called us, He gave us right standing with Him. And because He gave us right standing with Him, He also gave us His glory.

In Ephesians 3, Paul explains in a brilliant way his insight into the secret Christ Plan. By His Spirit, God has revealed this incredible secret plan to us. Jesus is the Building Plan according to which we are made new, from the inside out. Jesus is the solution to your brokenness—your rubble mess! Jesus is the vision, revelation, message, and blueprint God wants you to focus on. By grace, *our true identity is built into Christ.* In Christ all brokenness is repaired. In Him, you are continuously being rebuilt and restored for eternity!

Jesus reveals the following about our unity with Him and our unity with each other as He prays for the disciples, and also for you and me: "I am praying not only for these disciples but also for *all who will ever believe in me through their message.* I pray that they will all be one just as you and I are one—as you are in me, Father, and I am in you. And may they be in us so that the world will believe you sent me. I have given them the glory you gave me, so they may be one as we are one. I am in them and you are in me. May they experience such perfect unity that the world will know that you sent me and that you love them as much as you love me" (John 17:20–23, NLT).

This prayer of Jesus moves me in ways I can't even explain. To hear the Son of God, my Saviour, who was fully man yet fully God, *praying for me?*

Praying in the present tense. Still praying for me? And all of His children? All his disciples? Interceding for us? To know this intimate heart's desire of God. Everything Jesus said during his ministry on earth came directly from the Father (John 12:49). To hear how much emphasis God places on His children's perfect unity and to try and comprehend that God loves us as much as He loves Jesus... it blows my mind, expands my heart and ignites a passion to pursue this love and unity that connects me with God, with Jesus, and with fellow believers sharing in His glory!

This prayer of Jesus captures the essence of the entire building plan—for each individual person, as well as humanity as a unit. Jesus is our Mediator, our Bridge, High Priest, Salvation, Security, the only Way to our heavenly Father. When you accept Jesus as Saviour, you enter the new covenant with God where He looks at you and sees Jesus. He sees His promise and His plan. God made an oath that He'll never break (Hebrews 8:6–13). Even if we might fail God, He will never fail us!

He is moulding you with His righteousness, into His image and original plan. The Holy Spirit manages and oversees this building process with love and patience. Your spiritual healing and restoration are taking place, even when it's difficult to understand or put into words. You are covered in Christ's glory, even when you can't see it.

It's important to mention here that your salvation is received in a split second. Your eternal life with God is guaranteed the moment you believe that Jesus is the Son of God and that you need His saving grace (Ephesians 2:8). The criminal that hung next to Jesus on a cross, just asked Jesus to remember him when He got to heaven. He believed that Jesus could save him and bring him to heaven and Jesus responded that he would be with Him in paradise (Luke 23:43). He was saved by grace and by faith.

The spiritual growth process—the building process—takes longer than that moment of belief and even though it's not required to receive salvation, it stays important to God. It stays part of your temporary earthly existence. We are commanded by God to live holy (1 Peter 1:15–16), to be the salt and the light of the earth (Matthew 5:13–16), to love one another (John 13:34), to serve others (Galatians 5:13) and to bear the fruit of the Holy Spirit (Galatians 5:22–23).

Although we can't comprehend the reason we live on earth, for as long as we do, and though there may be times when we question the reason for our existence, with faith we have to hold on to what is written. Paul encourages us to press on like an athlete towards the finish line (2 Timothy 4:7). What doesn't make sense to us now, will make sense in eternity. Although we really want to focus on our own plans and dreams for our lives, and although we have received free will to creatively do our best with what we have been given, it has always been God's will that we do this *with* Him and *for* Him. When we truly realise that we don't belong to ourselves, but first and ultimately to God and then also to others, our priorities, needs, and ambitious striving will shift dramatically.

This truth will encourage you to embrace your unique design and to let go of the stressful striving to conform to the world's standards. The status quo will lose its value as your calling liberates your soul. There lies healing and restoration in the fulfilment of your heart's desires and ideas, which glorify God and build others up. More elaboration on Jesus as the Building Plan follows in the next chapter where we look at Christ as our Cornerstone.

The Holy Spirit as Builder and Site Manager of our lives:

John 14:26 (NLT): "But when the Father sends the Advocate as my representative—that is, the Holy Spirit—he will teach you everything and will remind you of everything I have told you."

In Chapter 8 we look at how the Holy Spirit fills us, moulds, builds, and maintains us, during this sanctifying process in which He transforms us into Christ's image, and restores God's image on earth. As the Holy Spirit builds Christ's church, He also guides and comforts us to find our true work-rest balance in God.

The Holy Spirit gives life and light to the building plan and makes it possible for us to be in Jesus Christ, as He is in God the Father. He understands the Christ Building Plan, always illuminating it. He builds us into a glorifying spiritual building. In the end, we can achieve nothing alone or by our own strength. We need the Holy Spirit! Zechariah 4:6 (NLT) "Then he said to me, 'This is what the Lord says to Zerubbabel: It is not by force nor by strength, but by my Spirit, says the Lord of Heaven's Armies'."

Build Me for Your Glory

I hand over my life, my control
To You, sovereign Lord, and Architect
To bring about Your original design
And to correct –
All the damages done;
The vast amount of neglect
How long will it take Lord?
You gently whisper: "We've only just begun."
You ask for participation –
Eager to share Your perfect plan
And vision of total repair
When You look at me
You see Christ's moulding –
A discipleship design unfolding...
Scars covering scars:
Brokenness healed by the breaking
Of Your own body, Your own heart
Providing hope, life and direction
Little by little approaching perfection
Fellowship will be restored forever
Streams of living water already sustain me,
Preserve me
You moisten this spirit to shape Your clay
From the inside out, You mould me
And shape me to portray:
Your Kingdom on earth:
A shadow of the one to come
A glorious promise and process
To take and change this mess
Back to Your original holy fortress.
Amen.

Chapter 4

God Our Rock, Christ Our Cornerstone

*Together, we are **his house**, built on the foundation of the apostles and the prophets. And the **cornerstone is Christ Jesus** Himself. We are carefully joined together in him, **becoming a holy temple** for the Lord. Through him you Gentiles are also being made part of this **dwelling where God lives by his Spirit**.*
—Ephesians 2:20–22 (NLT)

Life has sent your living stones tumbling and crumbling on many occasions. Problems, worries, and other builders have arrived—invited, and even uninvited—interfering with your walls, and chipping away with their building tools. Some stones lay splintered to pieces in the dirt and dust. Some are just too heavy to pick up again. Others again, just look too familiar to abandon. You pick them up with great nostalgia and effort to try and push them back into their old places—into those unstable spaces they just don't seem to quite fit. But you keep on trying...

At times, you've packed some of the old stones in the way they were before, using the knowledge you have and the memories you carry along. You have placed familiarity in front of risk. Sometimes it looked like it was working, at least for short periods of time. But again, and again, you've noticed that some stones are just not shaped to fit into the spaces you want them to fit. To force them in, just causes more pain.

These trying efforts to rebuild your walls over and over again by using your own strength—or what you have left of it—just to see the stones tumbling and breaking, have left you tired, frustrated, angry, irritated, and just mostly aching sore. Sore, because of the damage done. Sore, because of the impact. Sore, because of the feeling of rejection and abandonment when there wasn't a hand in sight to help you. Body-sore and soul-sore. That hopeless feeling overwhelms you, making you wonder if it could be depression. There's so much anger and frustration inside you. Without realising it, you're chiselling away at your own walls from the inside.

There comes a turning point in your life when you realise that you can't continue to push old stones back into their old places and just hope for the best. A turning point when the Building Team, the real Building Team, enters the scene and start the renovation process. The old walls simply won't work, they never did.

It's time that you go and find out why there are always cracks forming in your heart, relationships, and life. It's time that you start at the very beginning, completely over, the true way. That's the wonder of God's grace—always enough and always available for the willing heart that wants to try again. The Building Team is always ready for the next aspect that needs attention in this whole building process.

How does your foundation look? What are you currently building your life upon?

The purpose of a foundation is to provide a steady building platform on which a structure can be built, connecting the building structure to the ground as it carries the weight of the building to the ground. The strength of the building is also determined by the foundation. A foundation basically supports the entire structure built on it, keeps it standing safe and secure against outside forces and prevents ground moisture from seeping in and weakening the structure [3]

Matthew 7:24–27 (NLT): "Anyone who listens to my teaching and follows it is wise, like a person who builds a house on solid rock. Though the rain comes in torrents and the floodwaters rise and the winds beat against that house, it won't collapse because it's built on bedrock. But anyone who hears my teaching and doesn't obey it is foolish, like a person who builds a house on sand. When the rains and floods come and the winds beat against that house, it will collapse with a mighty crash."

Many verses in the Old Testament describe God as the unique God of Israel and as the Rock that provides shelter (Psalm 62:7, Psalm 28:1, Psalm 31:1–3, Psalm 61:2), security (2 Samuel 22:3, Psalm 18:2, Joel 3:16) and saves His children (Psalm 95:1, 2 Samuel 22:47, Psalm 18:46, Psalm 19:14, Psalm 62:2, Psalm 89:26, Isiah 17:10).

In Biblical times people literally built their houses with four sides and four corners on a quadrangle foundation wall of round uncut stones [34] They didn't have modern foundations of concrete as we know it today. The symbol of God as their Rock made complete sense to them, not only in terms of strength, shelter, and salvation, but as being a valuable anchor for their feet and homes.

The Holy of Holies part of the temple that was constructed on the Temple Mount, Mount Moriah, rested on rock of the mountain (2 Chronicles 3). God invites you to build your living stones, your whole life and being, on Him, the Rock of all ages. There is no other foundation for your existence. He is the starting point from the beginning of creation, leading to eternal sustainability. To accept God as your Rock, means to accept by faith that your life

---

[3] *htttps://sahomes.in/blog/the-importance-of-strong-foundations-for-buildings.*

[4] Wohlmanf-Kon, H. *DORleDOR. The world Jewish Bible Society. Jerusalem. Building in Biblical Times. p.1*

without Him is meaningless. He is the only One that saves and sustains you.

When you accept God as your Rock, you also acknowledge that there are no other foundations or beliefs on which to build your life. All other foundations are false and meaningless. God not only wants us to believe in His existence. He doesn't want your foundation exposed with no structure on it. It's His will for you to be built whole on Him and in Him. There's a reason for your existence. With God as your Rock, you will stand safe and secure when outside forces try to wreak havoc in your life. Anything that isn't from God, wouldn't be allowed to seep through to weaken or destroy you structure.

The only way then to build upon God as Rock, is to follow His building instructions and start at Jesus Christ as Cornerstone. Isaiah 28:16 (NLT): "Therefore, this is what the Sovereign Lord says: "Look! I am placing a foundation stone in Jerusalem, a firm and tested stone. It's a precious cornerstone that is safe to build on. Whoever believes need never be shaken.""

Where the Old Testament teaches us about God as the Rock that provides salvation, the New Testament elaborates on Jesus Christ as the Cornerstone that brings salvation. God's plan of salvation has thus never changed from the beginning, but came to fulfilment through Jesus.

Synonyms for cornerstone include: base, basis, bedrock, bottom, footing, foundation, ground, groundwork, keystone, root, and underpinning[5]. These synonyms display that the cornerstone and the foundation are united or built together.

Paul explains in 1 Corinthians 3:11 (NLT) how Jesus fits into God as Foundation: "For no one can lay any foundation other than the one we already have—Jesus Christ." In John 14:10–11 (NLT) Jesus asks: "Don't you believe that I am in the Father and the Father is in me? The words I speak are not my own, but my Father

---

[5] *https://www.merriam-webster.com/dictionary/cornerstone#synonyms*

who lives in me does His work through me. Just believe that I am in the Father and the Father is in me. Or at least believe because of the work you have seen me do." Furthermore, Jesus told the parable of the grapevine in John 15. Here Jesus explains that He is the true grapevine, God is the gardener and we are the branches that remain in Him.

The cornerstone is the first stone that is placed when building, influencing all the stones that follow as they are placed in line with the cornerstone. The cornerstone thus determines the position of the entire structure.

Living in modern times, cornerstones are now used differently. Foundations also looked different in Biblical times than the ones we see now. During Biblical times the cornerstone was the first stone that was placed within the foundation, making it the most important stone of the foundation. It was extremely important to place the cornerstone in the right place, level and straight, as it would determine the rest of the foundation and the structure being built on it.

What's the Bible revealing to us by referring to Jesus as the Cornerstone? Ephesians 2:20–22 (NLT): "Together, we are His house, built on the foundation of the apostles and the prophets. And the cornerstone is Christ Jesus Himself. We are carefully joined together in Him, becoming a holy temple for the Lord. Through Him you Gentiles are also being made part of this dwelling where God lives by His Spirit."

The prophets and apostles form part of the foundation (Ephesians 2:20) because their prophecies and teachings point towards and revolve around Jesus, the Cornerstone. They form the foundation of the church. With God as our Rock, Jesus as our Cornerstone and the rest of the foundation found within the teachings of the apostles, we have everything we need to be built into God's house. This building process brings us closer and closer to God. This building process is what our whole life is all about!

If God is our Rock and Jesus our Cornerstone, we can only

be built upon and within Him through His covenant with us in Jesus. A covenant is a contract between two parties. God promises everlasting life and salvation through Jesus Christ. It's a contract He initiated and has entered with us. To the human mind the concept of this contract is difficult to grasp. But by faith, we can receive the truth that when we decide to follow Jesus as The Way, we are in Christ, as He is in the Father. Romans 8:10–11 (NLT): "And Christ lives within you, so even though your body will die because of sin, the Spirit gives you life because you have been made right with God. The Spirit of God, who raised Christ Jesus from the dead, he will give life to your mortal bodies by this same Spirit living within you."

No matter how broken, dirty and messed up we are or how hard we wrestle with sin, we belong to God, and His salvation through Christ belongs to us even when we fail. When you accept Jesus as the Building Plan for your life, you won't be able to sin, build, and break as before. You will notice every skew stone that isn't placed in line with your Cornerstone, and it *will bother* you. Although you'll still be challenged by your sinful flesh, the enemy's deception, and worldly plans, the Holy Spirit you receive when you are born again of the spirit, will focus your eyes and heart on what is happening, bringing it into the light and into His truth.

We build our whole lives and relationship with God by starting at Jesus. Our broken walls just won't work for the kingdom of God. But in Jesus, despite our brokenness and damage, we are viewed as whole and righteous by God. That is why the Bible says Jesus is the only way to the Father. John 14:6–7 (NLT): "Jesus told him, "I am the way, the truth, and the life. No one can come to the Father except through me. If you had really known me, you would know who my Father is. From now on, you do know him and have seen him!"

Everything the prophets and apostles told us about Jesus, becomes part of our foundation of faith and the foundation of the body of Christ. Everything Jesus told us about Himself, the

Father, and Holy Spirit, shapes the outline of our foundation in God. When we build our lives upon God, we have the only strong and stabile foundation that will last eternally. Our walls won't ever tumble and crumble again. It doesn't help to believe in God but not believe in Jesus. Building our identity into Christ is the only way to God. It's also the only way to be built into a living temple with other believers.

Jesus is the Building Plan. The whole building starts with Jesus. *Your* whole building starts with Jesus.

The life that you build and the way the Holy Spirit builds you up, alongside, and together with other believers, starts with Jesus. When all your living stones are placed in line with Jesus, you become a spiritual house that fully reaches its potential and purpose.

Physically, there'll still be challenges from the outside—winds will shake your walls, unexpected storms will strike, and you will be exposed to earthly elements. Jesus never deceived anyone or promised a perfect life on earth once we follow Him and align our lives with Him. Jesus assured us that we *won't fit* in with worldly standards and that we *will* face persecution. We have a real enemy out there that will be banging against our walls harder than ever (1 Peter 5:8). But Jesus did promise us His peace during all of the chaos, joy through difficult times, and comfort in our sadness. He spoke about God's kingdom and promised that we'll eventually have a perfect life—the eternal life.

The sermon on the mount is one of the most challenging teachings of Jesus to grasp because it sounds so contradictory (Matthew 5:1–11). Although our earthly walls are exposed and influenced by the outside, we may know that our spiritual walls that are being built to stand steadfast throughout eternity, remain untouched and holy. Jesus' sermon on the mount challenges us in many ways to look at this temporary life with spiritual vision and to see the one beyond. Blessed are you when you accept and follow Jesus, because every challenge life will throw at you will only bring you closer to God and God's kingdom. Every stone of yours will be placed closer to His plan and laid down in His image, so no persecution or hardship will ever be able to take away your created purpose. To the contrary, every painful thing in this life will remind you of everything that Jesus has promised, increasing your hope and faith.

There's nothing on earth that can stop or destroy this spiritual building process. There's nothing that could ever separate you from His love and salvation (Romans 8:31–39). In faith, and with confidence, you can build with God. In your spirit, you will experience every step of the building process. And within this inner building process, you will experience the abundant life that Jesus promised (John 10:10). These inner changes will spill over to your external existence and will be seen and experienced by other people. It's the fruit we bear, the actions we take in faith, the serving contribution we make towards other's lives. It spills over into love. It's an incredible building process that'll never go unnoticed! Other people will not be able to help but notice the choices you're making with the guidance of the Holy Spirit. They won't be able to help but notice how your broken walls are being repaired. And that will bring glory to God. When your life brings glory to God, you are fulfilling your life's calling!

If you don't have Jesus as the Cornerstone of your life, all of your walls will be skew and uneven, crumbling, and leading to brokenness. When you don't start at Jesus Christ as Cornerstone, the whole position of your living structure will not be aligned with your life's calling and purpose.

Start to build again and don't stop. Begin to bring every living stone of your life in line with Jesus. Your spiritual house on the Rock, will stand strong and last for eternity!

Be my Cornerstone

As the builders rejected Your Cornerstone,
So, at times, have I
By following worldly passions and ambitions—mine
Moving away from Your righteous plumb line
I've ended up building skew walls –
Painful protruding stones and spiritual spirals
Dust rising, eyes stinging,
Prideful pieces crumbling, falling –
Exposing a foundation full of flaws, unevenness
Which lead to this vulnerable soul barrenness
Begin again, Oh Lord –
The only true and everlasting foundation
Lay Your Cornerstone with this redeemed transformation,
Your Spirit, Your hand in mine
I am not alone
As I partake in the process You align
Plumb line perfection pursued
With Your just measure line
It hurts but it heals
I am alive, revived, excited for the final reveal
When the capstone will be placed
Your master plan at last complete
Forever in Your holy presence
Built into Your heavenly kingdom, its very essence!
Amen.

PART 2
STRUCTURE

Chapter 5

Building Dust of Discipleship

*So why do you keep calling me 'Lord, Lord!' when you don't do what I say? I will show you **what it's like when someone comes to me, listens to my teaching, and then follows it. It's like a person building a house who digs deep and lays the foundation on solid rock.** When the floodwaters rise and break against that house, it stands firm because it's **well built**. But anyone who hears and doesn't obey is like a person who builds a house right on the ground, without a foundation. When the floods sweep down against that house it will collapse into a heap of ruins.*
—Luke 6:46–49 (NLT)

You stand in awe on the construction site as you take it all in. Gratefulness floods your soul. For the first time the foundation is perfect and stabile. You feel anchored, secure, and reassured. Safe. What a great relief that the great rubble mess has been removed.

It's a process.

The site under construction looks more like organised chaos. The big eyesore of a gap has been closed up neatly, mysteriously filled. Curiously you move over the new solid foundation. As you're moving, your mind is beginning to grasp the layout of the Building Plan—even if it's only partially. You see the layout of your Building Team's vision. You're starting to get an idea of the structure that

65

needs to be built on this foundation. You feel hopeful and even excited! A great expectation has been created in your whole being! You experience *hope*.

The moment feels so overwhelming that you go onto your knees. But you want to move even closer. You lie down flat on the foundation, face down, arms outstretched, embracing, and lovingly submitting.

Pain and cries for help covered the previous shaky foundation. Now, in its place, worship is overflowing. While you are in this position of worship, your fingers lightly stroke the stones, packed so perfectly...

It's a love embrace and acceptance. It's a never-look-back-realisation and a never-build-differently-promise taking place.

With an open heart, open arms, and open hands, you move back onto your knees and crawl towards the Cornerstone. This is the most important stone of your entire building, your whole reason for existence. It's at the Cornerstone that you sit down to talk, to pray, to beg, and to ask God: *"How do we build on this?"* It's by examining the Cornerstone, that you will find clear indications and instructions for the building process to follow. That *you* will follow.

The Cornerstone tells you everything. He has already determined everything and has everything under control. The Cornerstone is built into your own being. With the Rock-solid foundation firmly in place, the Cornerstone now demonstrates to you how the rest of the building needs to be constructed. With the Cornerstone perfectly formed and perfectly laid down, your building structure will be nothing less than completely accurate, righteous, straight, and level—as long as you start at the Cornerstone.

The Cornerstone is Jesus Christ. The construction of the building, in line with Christ, is therefore nothing other than the *process of discipleship*. To follow Christ means to be a disciple (Matthew 4:19). God's plan for your restoration, the Christ building plan, is fulfilled by the Holy Spirit's work in you, transforming you into a living spiritual building. The Holy Spirit Who dwells in you and is building you up in Jesus Christ, brings shape to your building through the process of discipleship, always pointing to Christ and glorifying God.

Discipleship isn't meant for *certain* believers. Everyone who believes in Jesus, is called to be His disciple and to live out the process of discipleship for the rest of their lives. If you truly follow Jesus, your faith in Him will be visible in acts of discipleship. If you're wondering whether you truly believe and whether you're truly building in line with the Cornerstone, ask yourself if you are obeying Jesus' commandments. To believe in Jesus but not do what He says, isn't faith at all. Faith without works is dead (James 2:26).

Faith in Jesus, without discipleship, is dead.

Bill Hull defines a disciple as a reborn follower and learner of Jesus Christ. He also goes on to say that there is no Biblical evidence that the word Christian and disciple are used in two different ways. Rather, every normal Christian should be viewed as a disciple[6].

Michael Wilkins, New Testament Professor of Language and Literature at Talbot School of Theology, explains that the term "disciple" is used as the primary term in the Gospels to refer to all the followers of Jesus in the first church. That included all types of followers, even when they were referred to as believers, Christians, brothers and sisters, those of the way, or saints. These referring terms explained the context of each person's individual relationship with Jesus and other believers, but they were still viewed as disciples[7].

You are reborn to be made a disciple. It's not an optional

---

[6] *Hull, B. The Complete Book of Discipleship. On being and making followers of Christ, p32*

[7] *Hull, B. The Complete Book of Discipleship. On being and making followers of Christ, p32*

choice and there are no various sections of Christianity where some believers become disciple, and others don't. By studying God's Word, it becomes clear that discipleship is inseparably part of Christianity and the only true process that can be followed when you decide to follow Jesus. It's also not the case that you make decisions in your faith according to steps. You don't become a reborn Christian and then decide whether you want to become a disciple or not. When you are born again and when you receive the Holy Spirit, you immediately enter the discipleship process, and your true identity in Christ is immediately restored.

You immediately lay down your previous worldly building plan in exchange for God's building plan, the Christ Plan. From that moment, you receive righteousness, and the Holy Spirit starts to renovate you into Christ's image, journeying with you as He sanctifies you and glorifies God. This glory will reach its final completion in eternity but already starts here on earth. A little bit of heaven is already gracefully revealed to us.

2 Corinthians 3:18 (NLT) says it like this: "So all of us who have had the veil removed can see and reflect the glory of the Lord. And the Lord—who is Spirit—makes us more and more like him as we are changed into his glorious image."

Do you see yourself being made more and more into His image, to reflect His glory?

This process of being made into Christ's image, His nature, His character and His Spirit, is marked by progress and not perfection[8]. It's a lifelong process of becoming a disciple. It provides meaning to this life that we sometimes experience as meaningless. There's a reason and a purpose for your life. There's a reason and a purpose for today. There's a reason and a purpose that we can't see with our natural eyes or understand by using our natural senses.

---

[8] *Hull, B. The Complete Book of Discipleship. On being and making followers of Christ, p33*

You can experience the weight, of the expectation to instantly reflect Christ's image, lifted from your shoulders.

It's allowed to take time. It's supposed to take time. God designed the discipleship process to be a *process*; and a process *requires time*. The New Testament testifies about it. The disciples of Jesus had to spend a lot of time with Him to learn from Him and follow Him.

Every believer will grow from an infant-like believer into a mature believer (Hebrews 5:12). Both parts of this lengthy process are important. Discipleship isn't a choice or an option. Discipleship is the Holy Spirit's building process, transforming faith into deeds and cultivating spiritual fruit that grow and multiply.

Discipleship is part of the sanctifying and glorifying process that the Holy Spirit uses to build your spiritual building in line with Jesus, the Cornerstone of the entire spiritual building. In this process that you are being built, aligned with Christ on God the Rock, you will be reflecting more and more of God's image. It's when you are in Christ, like Christ is in God, that God's image on earth is lived out in such a way that it glorifies Him most.

It's not an isolated process. It's meant to take place in relationship with other disciples of Christ. That is what the amazing revelation in Ephesians 2:19–22 is all about! What this book you are holding now is all about!

When we realise that there's no difference between a Christian and a disciple, the unity within the body of Christ is strengthened and becomes fully functional.

Every Christian is a disciple. You are a disciple. I am a disciple. Together we form the members of Christ's body. Together we perform the function of discipleship.

One of the wonders of the body of Christ is that every member stays unique. Every normal Christian stays a unique person. You are allowed to live out your calling in your unique way within the greater body. We don't need to all look or act the same.

Our purpose to reflect Christ's image unites our unique callings.

The type of disciple you are may differ from another disciple. Personality, temperament, culture, and passions influence us to serve the body of Christ in various ways. While we make our unique contributions, our goal will remain the same—to follow Christ's character and example as close as possible while we serve and love one another.

One disciple may serve lovingly by preparing a meal and another by giving a donation. Some might prefer to organise a gathering or function, and another would like to lead worship, or exhort another believer with words of encouragement. Some will display great hospitality, while others will want to share what they have, or make something creative to the benefit of another believer. Some will want to provide gentle comfort during distress, while another feels more comfortable to motivate energetically. Our diverse personalities and gifts should strengthen our unity rather than cause division among members. It's supposed to draw us closer to one another, because we are all in need of the gifts that we receive from one another. How we serve in our unique way is completely good and essential, as long as we do it out of love for God and other believers, with the purpose to glorify God and build up the body of Christ.

The only way to know whether we're busy reflecting Christ's image or not, is to spend personal time with Him in prayer and by studying God's Word. When we study the Gospels, we learn more and more about Jesus' focus, thoughts, words, actions, emotions, teachings, and Spirit. As you learn more about Jesus, you will also learn more about God the Father.

Jesus said in John 12:49 that everything He says comes directly from the Father. Jesus showed us what it looks like to live according to God, our heavenly Father's, image.

What does it mean to follow Jesus? What does it mean to be transformed from glory to glory? What exactly does this building plan of God, the Christ Plan, entail? We have to make a personal study of the life of Jesus. We have to examine our Cornerstone up close and make personal contact with Him. Jesus showed us how to serve and love one another, how to pray, what to do with finances, where our focus must lie in the things we seek, how to thank and praise God, which glorifying characteristics to develop, and all the fleshly desires we need to resist. These are just a few examples.

The biggest element that stands out in Jesus' life and ministry is the command to love. Matthew 22:37–40 (NLT): "Jesus replied, You must love the Lord your God with all your heart, all your soul and all your mind. This is the first and greatest commandment. A second is equally important: 'Love your neighbour as yourself.' The entire law and all the demands of the prophets are based on these two commandments". And in John 13:34–35 (NLT) Jesus also said: "So now I am giving you a new commandment: Love each other. Just as I have loved you, you should love each other. Your love for one another will prove to the world that you are my disciples".

The greatest way to follow Jesus and show that we are His disciples is by living a life of love—all-encompassing love for God and genuine love for people. Our passionate love for God will automatically lead to love for people as we'll start to reflect God's image of love.

It's impossible to love God but not love people. It's also not easy loving people earnestly, without loving God first.

This type of love will also help us to live out all of the other functions of discipleship. It will transform you into a servant of God and a servant of people. Jesus showed us what it looks like to serve and humble ourselves, always giving God the credit and honour for His works. Jesus got really close to people. Jesus connected with people.

Jesus touched dirty feet, sick bodies, and had personal conversations. Jesus got personal. Being a disciple means we need to step out of our comfort zone, subdue our anxious flesh, and get personal with other people. Jesus' focus was always on the kingdom of God. Every parable and deed revolved around it. Jesus encouraged us to gather treasures in heaven and to focus on salvation and relationships rather than earthly possessions (Matthew 6:19–20).

One of the most challenging parts that stand out in being a true disciple of Jesus, is the willingness to leave behind a worldly lifestyle. We need to be willing to be selfless, deny ourselves, and sacrifice anything that stands in our way of being a true disciple (Luke 17:33). There's nothing wrong with needing the essentials for survival, and Jesus taught us to trust that God would always provide what is necessary (Matthew 6:8). But we must be willing to pick up our cross daily, the battle and sacrifices in our daily living, in order to follow Him. We truly need to be willing to lay down our lives for Him, for our faith in Him, and even be willing to lay it down for another person. We need to be willing to face persecution and be unpopular. Tough call!

But God's entire Word is the truth—we can't decide which parts we'll accept and incorporate into our faith and daily living and which parts we choose to view as only symbolic or irrelevant.

Sure, we need to study the Bible and gain an understanding of the context of what is revealed. God says that as we grow in faith and pursue His Word, His Truth, even more insight will be given to us. As we grow in our faith and identity in Christ, we are given more wisdom and understanding of His Word (Matthew 13:10–12). We get to a place where we realise, we need to accept the entire truth of God's Word and actually really do what Jesus told His disciples to do—what He is still telling us to do! His Word is alive! He is speaking to you. There are no if's or but's.

To follow Jesus, is amazing beyond words yet very challenging. That's why Jesus said we need to count the cost before we decide to follow Him. Why would He say that it would cost you, if it was only going to be wonderful, peaceful, and comfortable? Luke 14:27–29, TPT: "And anyone that comes to me must be willing to share my cross and experience it as his own, or he cannot be considered to be my disciple. So don't follow me without considering the cost you. For who would construct a house before first sitting down to estimate the cost to complete it? Otherwise he may lay the foundation and not be able to finish..."

If we take God's entire Word seriously, if we take Jesus seriously, we really need to do what He taught us to do and serve in the way He displayed it for us. We need to experience His cross as our own to receive salvation, but we also need to copy His actions to be true disciples. We need to care for the widows and the orphans. We need to give to the government what belongs to the government and to God what belongs to God. We need to share what we have to help someone in need. We need to invite people over for dinner that we feel uncomfortable to invite, due to their status. We need to resist temptations. We need to pray and fast. We need to be filled with the Holy Spirit. We need to stop our rushing, put agendas aside when God sends someone on our path, connect with that person, and prioritize relationships. We need to distance ourselves from the things God hates—the things that grieve the Holy Spirit. We need to resist temptations and conquer addictions. We need to be in control of our flesh. We need to tell people about Jesus, set the captives free and let our lights shine in the darkness. We need to forgive our enemies and even *pray* for them! We do!

Go and study God's Word, study Jesus. Look at Jesus, with the realisation of the truth that you are His disciple. Look at Him as your Teacher... and do what He teaches you to do. Don't get deceived or overcomplicate things. Stand in the truth; live in the truth; share the truth.

Another fleshly challenge to overcome as we receive Jesus' cross, is to move aside the approval of people and to rather seek the approval of God. *A human being's approval is only temporary. God's approval lasts for eternity.*

It's not an easy path to follow, but the heavenly rewards are much greater than the temporary sacrifices. Jesus played open cards with us, never hiding the consequences and sacrifices required when we decide to follow Him. The price is high—it covers your entire life, and in extreme cases your life itself, but the reward in heaven is greater! (Matthew 5:12).

The essence of one of John Piper's books, *Don't waste your life,* is that we are created in God's image to represent God's image on earth and to do it in such a way that God receives the glory for it. We are not just created in God's image, we are created *in* His images *and for* His glory (Genesis 1:27). We didn't receive this wonderful authority over creation and all these creative abilities, just to simply represent God's image on earth. Everything we do must *also bring glory* to God!

How do you know whether your actions are glorifying God? When people not only need and appreciate your gifts and talents, but thank God for what *He* is doing in their lives *through you.* Your life glorifies God when people not only see what you do, but notice or grasp the Christ-centred reason for your actions. God is glorified when people give God the credit for our actions. We might not even know about these glorifying moments taking place silently within the hearts that move and beat around us. This shouldn't stop us from using every moment and opportunity to reflect and honour God with our thoughts, words, and actions.

Our purpose as image-bearers is always to move the attention away from ourselves and to magnify God's glory. We need to live Christ-magnifying lives that make other glad in Christ[9]. And when will people be thanking God for what you're doing? When you humbly give God all the honour and credit, while living a life that testifies your dedication towards Him. People will thank God when they experience that the things they receive from your heart and hands, are in reality God's love and care for them.

You are a vessel of so many great characteristics of God! You

---

[9] Piper, J. Don't waste your life, p.66

were created to shift the focus towards God, so that His image is glorified.

People will always give honour to other people by handing over awards, prizes, gifts, and by placing them on a platform in public where the tokens of appreciation can be seen and acknowledged. How amazing that God doesn't honour Himself by specifically appointing only certain people to publicly give Him honour and acknowledgement in that way. He uses normal people like you and me to honour Him by the lives we are living! God took the risk of placing normal people in the position of highlighting His glory to the world. Anything and everything we do, must reflect God's character and nature in such a way that others will give God the glory for it. Otherwise, you are just wasting your life.

You can't choose where, when, and how you'll represent God's image. You can't decide where you want to commit yourself completely, and where you want to enjoy your freedom in areas of your life that will never glorify God. You can't customise the discipleship process to be make it more comfortable or pleasurable. That is *not* true discipleship.

This command to bring glory to God, is always meant to make other people aware of God and to make *them* glad in God. It's never about what's in it for you. Glorifying actions are meant to be experienced and shared with other people. It's meant to build up the body parts of Christ so that every part of the body, in unity, can display a greater glorifying image of God. It's in this unity that God's temple and dwelling place is formed. Every part of the body of Christ shows a unique part of God's image. That is why we should never compare ourselves or look down on one another. Each person's reflection plays an important part and without all the various parts, we won't be able to see the greater picture of God's image on earth.

Jesus' life resembles a perfect example of one that represents and magnifies God's image, bringing glory and honour to God. John 10:30 (NLT): "The Father and I are one." Even though it's not possible for us with our fallen nature to be exactly like Jesus, it remains God's will that we live as His disciples and follow Him as close as possible. That is why He sent the help of the Holy Spirit. According to God's Word, we've already received all of Christ's glory and all the heavenly treasures in Christ. The Holy Spirit within us guides us and forms us closer and closer to His image. He is taking us from glory to glory (2 Corinthians 3:18).

The Holy Spirit helps you to strive for discipleship as the building process during the construction of His dwelling place. It's not to be taken lightly. It's not enough to just know about Jesus, His teachings, and His ministry. We need to work together to be disciples. Our own discipleship process needs to lead to action, making and refining disciples around us. Discipleship isn't a legalistic approach to Christianity. If a normal Christian is a disciple, then Christianity is equal to discipleship.

Discipleship isn't a structure of rules and loveless obligations, it's a spiritual growth process that develops within relationship.

Live out your building process of discipleship in such a way that it helps other believers along in the same process. Let your building process also provide encouragement, guidance, and an example to those that are lost. Without always realising, you are busy displaying discipleship wherever you move.

Be careful how you build on the discipleship layout provided by the apostles and the prophets (Ephesians 2:20). To only believe in God, but not build on Him, actually testifies of unbelief. Does your discipleship build others up and lead them closer to Christ's image? Or is it a dead-end process that is stuck, unable to progress, a foundation without a structure?

Or are the building dust particles of Jesus Christ busy covering your life to such an extent that some of it is even landing on the people around you?

Dust...

As You align my stones with Yours
My feet following Your course
My heart beats with Yours: duplicated
And to my surprise I feel completely liberated!
Though I follow, I am free
Because in You
I fully become who I was meant to be
As I listen and I learn
I grow and I yearn
For more...
More meaning, hope, and truth—the core,
The centre, essence, of the cross
Coating me:
Providing identity
Closely treasured and carried to eternity,
With my eyes focused on Your kingdom route
I'll follow each step so closely –
The dust of Your feet covering me.
Amen.

Chapter 6

Stay on the Wall – Distractions and Opposition

But I realised they were plotting to harm me, so I
*replied by sending this message to them: **I am engaged***
***in a great work, so I can't come.** Why should I*
stop working to come and meet with you?
—*Nehemiah 6:2–3 (NLT)*

The building process feels never-ending. For a moment, you step back to view the bigger picture that has been created up until this present moment. You see some structure taking form, but you also see that this building is far from finished. Honestly, you are extremely exhausted...

You also face the temptation to turn your back, if only for a little while, just to focus on something else for a change. To just walk away for a short while. To break the intensity of it all. Maybe you can return once you feel ready again? Can you afford to let the building project stand still for a short time?

This discipleship process is all-consuming and there are stones within you that you're not ready to throw on the dumping site yet.

A few times, you've even gone back to the rubble heap to collect some precious old stones. You carried these old stones back to your new building, almost feeling a bit nostalgic—longing for the comfort they had once provided. It's easy to forget the discomfort and damage they've actually caused. You've even tried, in a subtle way, to pack these stones back into your new building, hoping no one would notice them. Hoping your Building Team would overlook it. But you can't fool them. And you can't even fool yourself anymore. That's the thing—your conscience is suddenly so awake and active. No ignorance. No bliss.

Your Building Team is patient. They do things right and don't miss a single thing you think or do. With irritation and frustration, you ask them—and yourself—why they don't just destroy these old stones completely? Why keep it close by, where you are constantly reminded of it, and always have access to it? Why allow all these free choices? Why are there still so many temptations?

All these meetings, just to stay on the same page with your Building Team, gets overwhelming at times. You have a lot to process. You even wonder if the Building Team gets tired of you throughout this process. Actually, they are so patient and confident, even too patient for your liking! There are times when you're actually incredibly grateful for the *pace*—and the *breathing space* they allow and provide.

Things just aren't always taking place as fast as you would like it to. It feels like you'll never get to where you're supposed to be. It's difficult to see how much change has taken place. Things still look so messy. You are frustrated. You feel guilty. You're trying to be thankful. Trying to be patient. But you get angry!

You're not even exactly sure who you're angry with—yourself, the people that participated in creating your big original gap mess, the other distracting builders around you, or even your Building Team. Maybe you're just angry at everything and everyone at once! It's with a feeling of shame that you admit to yourself—you don't always like your Building Team. It's not that you don't like them, it's their *process* that you don't always like. The inconsistency of your own soul, might even frustrate you more than anything else.

There are times when you understand the Christ Plan and visualise its outlines. It even inspires you to press towards the goal. Some days you even experience real joy. Other days the joy feels absent or very weak. Maybe you're struggling to comprehend what *joy* really is. You do however experience some form of contentment as your faith increases. You wish you could offer more gratitude, praise, and joy to your Building Team, knowing full well that you actually don't deserve any of their grace and goodness...

But on the days when the winds of exhaustion are threatening to knock your structure down, everything gets foggy, and it feels like you forget. But you can't truly forget and *that* makes you even more tired. Because sometimes, you just prefer to forget. Sometimes you just want to go and sit inside your dust bubble and think of nothing. And sometimes you just want to pull your old stones closer and embrace them for a while. There are so many memories, so many people, so many feelings... You try to convince yourself that not all of them are bad memories, that there's nothing wrong with looking at your old stones.

Take a good long look at them. But when you look, also remember in what condition you were found and saved. See them. But also see how far you've already come. Can you really identify with these old stones? Do you even want to? Will they ever have a place in the new building structure?

Are you imagining it, or do you hear another voice defending your pity party? The voice sounds so satisfying—telling you exactly what you want to hear in moments like these. However, something about the voice makes you feel uncomfortable. It's impossible to listen to two voices at the same time. You can't perform two different tasks at the same time. Ever since the Holy Spirit has moved into your building and started building with you, it has become easier to identify *the echo of the false truth* and the glow of the *false light*.

The Holy Spirit is your Helper and Comforter (John 14:26). He doesn't abandon you for a second and keeps on pointing out the truth (John 16:13). The radiance of His light is so much brighter than the false light.

It doesn't help to close your eyes and block your ears. It didn't help in the first place—why would it now? Even when you disappoint the Holy Spirit, He never leaves or forsake you. He is now part of this building and this building is you.

When you listen to the wrong voice, the building process slows down and you can sense the atmosphere of the building site being filled with grief. A terrible tangible darkness is experienced in your core. During these experiences, you thought that the Holy Spirit would leave, but every time you've seen Him sitting with you in and through the dark chaos. Sometimes it gets so dark, that you can't even see Him properly. It's only when you allow His light to conquer the darkness and reveal the truth, that you notice He hasn't moved away. He grieves (Ephesians 4:30), and He waits, until you are ready to continue building. How will our minds ever comprehend this dedication and love?

On top of your own construction noise, you also hear other noises and voices coming from the outside. There are people who notice your frustration. Oh boy, but do they miss you. Out of their own pure frustration, they have walked away from their construction site.

They arrive at your property—restless. You can identify so well with each other's dissatisfaction. This life and this building process can be so hard. Their empathy is like plasters on your sore fingers. So sore from all the hard labour. They keep on inviting you to visit them while they also continue to build, and break, and wait. Maybe just to rest with them. To just let go with them— for the company and for the fun. They also experience intense loneliness inside their own building.

They offer you refreshment in the shadows of their own crooked walls.

The false voice is trying to convince you that these crooked walls don't look too bad. Maybe it's just...different? What's wrong with different? "Life is really hard and certainly everybody can't follow the same building plan. Is there anyway a real blueprint? A unity for all?", the voice with the uncomfortable echo whispers.

The true voice, which you by now distinguish as your conscience through which the Holy Spirit speaks to you, tells you that it might not look that bad, but that it's definitely not right. You remember everything you learned about the Foundation and the Cornerstone. You see trouble on the way with that building style.

You still wonder what damage it could cause to move away from your building site for a little while. What exactly would happen if you turned away for a moment? Maybe you could even succeed in helping this other builder to build according to the right plan. You're not sure if the person would be open for your advice or if the conversation would move towards that subject. It's uncomfortable for both parties—the possible confrontation. You're aware of the truth that you would have to tell them about breaking down their skew walls, to start over, and build on the right foundation. Not everybody is willing.

You aren't always aware of the fact that it makes things much more difficult for yourself—when your building process slows down or stands still. You don't know who's hanging around your construction site, ready to vandalise and break down what you have worked very hard on to build up. You don't realise that you expose yourself to the unknown when you lose focus. Being so tired, you're vulnerable to receive deceptive advice that may cause confusion—another few uneven stones that will need to be painfully chiselled out of your building.

You remember a previous time that you wanted to relax for a while at another builder's site. You knew that builder was making a big mess out of their building. But it hasn't always looked like a mess before. It looked like a familiar style—it looked like your own previous one. You wanted to be part of their life yet separate. That was your sincere plan. Before you knew it, some of their stones came tumbling down and injured you. Not only did you return the next day to your own construction site with an injured soul, but some pieces of their stones fell into your overalls and ended up being built into your new walls. It was painful to repair that part of your wall again. You remember the laborious smoothing out...

Disheartened, you collapse against one of your new walls. It feels smooth, straight, strong, and stable. But you still experience frustration. The temptations within still surface. Everyone is building so loudly around you. The world makes a big noise and keeps on distracting you. Thoughts get lost and prayers interrupted...

The Building Team is so full of mercy and grace. They listen to you and provide the opportunity for you to process what is on your foreground. They never force you to move beyond the pace that you can handle. It makes you feel guilty. It also makes you feel incredibly grateful. No matter how hard it is, you know for sure that you need to focus your attention on the building process. You remember everything the Building Team has told you. They never provided false hope or detours. They were honest about the process and keep on reminding you of their promise to never forsake or reject you (Hebrews 13:5, John 10:29). They even encourage you to rest by them (Matthew 11:28). To rest *by* them, *not rest from* the project. Don't quit the project, stay on board. Rest is part of the project, as we will explore in Chapter 8.

Faith provides the power needed to rise again. Omnipresent and extraordinarily wise, your Building Team lifts up your head and readjusts your focus. They teach you where your focus needs to lie.

And now you see them—all the other builders that are facing the *same* battles. You notice all the other builders next to you that are also building on the Rock and following the Christ Plan. You are not alone. And you can choose with whom you want to share your battle. You remember that you're not supposed to get caught up in your own building, all alone. You've reached the point where you *want* to build. You also want to help others build.

Your neighbour's walls are being built right up against yours.

You're connected. They provide so much support to your own building. Your unity strengthens one another. You don't need to abandon your building process to seek company. There are people right next to you that want to help you carry your burdens and also celebrate your progress. Your joy is shared. You have the same end goal in sight. You even help each other to stay focused and prevent the return to the rubble heap on the dumpsite.

You have the same Building Team! How's it possible for them to be so powerful and omnipresent? It amazes each builder! The same Spirit lives in each structure that is being built according to the Christ Plan. There's a love and shared peace that invisibly connects you to each other. You're amazed to hear about the same false voice echoing through their buildings as well. You are stunned by the fact that they also sometimes struggle to function in a deceptively dim light. No one faces this battle alone.

As you look at your neighbour, you realise it's easier to build together with one another and right next to each other. You really want to encourage your family and friends to build with you! The unity among the builders strengthens everyone, and suddenly everyone receives so much more input from the Building Team than they could've on their own. You even hear about each other's meetings with the Building Team. These testimonies are treasures. Together you are beginning to gain a much greater in depth understanding of their vision.

It's within this relationship with your Building Team and your relationship with other fellow builders—who are also in relationship with the Building Team—that a powerful unity of strength is formed. A unity that is able to provide true resistance. Together, we can say "no" more easily to temptations. Together, we can pray for each other, encourage one another, and stand firm against the onslaught of attacks coming from outside our walls. Together, challenges are faced—of not fitting in with the world and not building according to worldly plans. Together, our faith is strengthened and our gifts from the Holy Spirit provide everything that we need to press on and build His kingdom! Together, we can rest safely and together, we can celebrate and praise our Building Team! Together, we can listen to the Building Team and discuss what to pursue and what to avoid by studying God's Word. It's within these valuable times of fellowship, teaching, and connecting, that we can look in depth at what is written.

Together, we can look at books like Nehemiah and learn so much from it. While Nehemiah was busy managing the repair of Jerusalem's walls, the Jews' enemies pretended to be friends. They invited him over for a meeting—not only once, but four times. God gave Nehemiah discernment to identify this as a trap. In reality, they were false friends, only trying to distract Nehemiah from his important assignment and trying to stop the building of Jerusalem's walls from progressing.

Nehemiah 6:2–4 (NLT): "So Sanballat and Geshem sent a message asking me to meet them at one of the villages in the plain of Ono. But I realised they were plotting to harm me, so I replied by sending this message to them: "I am engaged in a great work, so I can't come. Why should I stop working to come and meet with you?" Four times they sent the same message, and each time I gave the same reply."

After this had taken place, we learn that the enemy started to send threats in Nehemiah 6:8–9 (NLT): "I replied, 'There is no truth in any part of your story. You are making up the whole thing.' They were just trying to intimidate us, imagining that they could discourage us and stop the work. So, I continued the work with even greater determination.'"

You know exactly what threats and challenges are being sent your way to distract and demotivate you. You can identify the people and tasks at hand that are busy inviting you into temptation or intimidating you in order to slow down or even stop your building process. You know your old stones and recognise the new ones being promoted by false friends. You know which enemies want to break down your walls, and who or what is trying to break in—only to put chains on you again.

Many times, the pressure is coming from people or sinful things from the outside, but it can also come from within, when we battle with our own sinful nature. Sometimes, we don't even realise that we've become our own enemy. We need the Holy Spirit's guidance and other believers' input to stay on course and to ensure that we're also providing support to our fellow-builders.

Be like Nehemiah. Be alert and focused. The Building Team has entrusted you with an exceptional building project. Don't walk away from the process until the capstone is placed. Press on and be aware of every lie and distracting task that is trying to prevent you from reaching your purpose. Be ready with your answer that you can't attend whatever is stealing your time and attention away from living out your calling. Be ready to say that *you* are busy with very important work. Pray and ask God for the strength needed so the building work can continue. Build in unity with your fellow builders in the battle.

Fervently Focused

My eyes shift from You –
To the work You have assigned
Back and forth
I will not lose focus
The battle is real and outlined
Not against flesh and blood –
Requiring spiritual refocus
Awake and alert:
Both weapon and building equipment
I will assert,
Not losing grip
Quickly arising when I trip –
Always adjusting and readjusting
But never forgetting or compromising
Resisting the enemy
As I pursue this God-given calling,
The stakes are high at times
And energy low
But with Your spirit I overcome each blow
In my weakness, You are strong –
Helping me discern right from wrong
I press on towards the end goal:
Sanctified, restored, and whole.
Amen.

Chapter 7

Building Equipment and Gear

*The laborers carried on their work with **one hand***
***supporting their load** and **one hand holding a weapon**.*
***All the builders had a sword belted to their side**.*
*The trumpeter stayed with me to sound the **alarm**.*
—*Nehemiah 4:17–18 (NLT)*

The construction site creates a busy and dusty environment. You look at your calloused hands and pull uncomfortably on your overalls. You didn't realise the Building Team was going to make you work this hard and trust you with these many responsibilities. You kind of hoped they would do most of the work themselves. Maybe you've always had a misconception about what they should or would do for you—a misconstruction dilemma.

Up until now, you've never fully realised that to be built into this discipleship structure, would require of you to follow through with *all* the instructions that the Building Team provides. You've also seen that to sit, wait, and watch what will happen while you do nothing, leads to exactly that—nothing. Nothing happens without your cooperation and input. Free will's function only makes sense to you now, and you are stunned that God trusts you with this amount of freedom and choices. Because, if you really want to throw in the rope and turn your back on this difficult process, you may.

It's your choice if you want to resist this whole transformation process.

But it will bother you because of the new heart and spirit you have received the day you signed the contract. Ever since you've accepted the Christ Plan, your building is being filled continuously with the presence of the Holy Spirit. He is the Builder within you, guiding each action, and always glorifying Christ. He always points to the Christ Plan. He never judges, He only convicts, making sure you're building according to the Word's plumb line.

The Holy Spirit provides all the tools necessary for this project. He encourages and equips, but never forces or dominates. When you refuse to listen to Him, it grieves Him tremendously. But He is faithful. He never abandons or rejects you. To the contrary, He is your greatest Comforter.

Your building has been sealed by Him. You belong to God. Even if you make mistakes, even if you mess up badly, nothing can break the covenant contract you're in. Nothing can separate you from Him or tear you away from His foundation. No matter the amount of renovation and reconstruction required, He's always there to help you. He keeps pointing to the Christ Plan when you're tempted to go back to the dumpsite. Even though this isn't exactly what you expected, you know this is the only way, and you're filled with hope to see the final reveal.

Sometimes you get so busy and tired that you forget to put on the right clothing gear for the project. Other times, you just grab your trowel but forget your weapon. Some days you take chances to enter the construction site without the right safety gear. There are also days when you just simply stand right next to the site when you have absolutely no gear on. The Holy Spirit teaches you everything and guides you in all truth (John 16:13).

The Building Team has informed you about all the rules and regulations. They have equipped you with everything you need. You have been geared with the right clothes and tools to ensure your optimal and safe participation in the process. Sometimes you forget the importance of it all, only to afterwards experience the damage done to your body, soul and spirit.

You are busy learning and training how to use your weapon and tools—thankful for all the grace and chances that you receive to try over and over again. Here and there, you still make mistakes, but you also learn from them and try to repair them. It's all part of the building and breaking of the discipleship process. Honesty, is the only way to deal with your mistakes now. Your Architect already sees everything you're doing. It doesn't help to even try and hide it. Grace upon grace you receive, over and over again because your Architect knows your heart, and knows His promise. An incredible relationship is being built, and you feel safe with Him. Shy and embarrassed at times, but always safe.

You're even busy learning to extend the same type of grace that you've received for your mistakes, to your fellow builders. Every day, you realise more and more, how hard this building process is, and how far all the builders fall short.

It has always been easier to criticise from the side line... until the day you had to get your own hands dirty. That day, everything changed. Your vision is being expanded to such a great extend to fit your Architect's plan, that you are starting to look at your fellow builders with new eyes. Awe-struck you wonder how the Architect is able to coordinate everyone with their unique building styles.

The end product looks the same, but everyone is being accommodated in a unique way throughout the whole process. Nowadays you pray for wisdom, and hold emergency meetings with your Architect about all the chaos that you see and struggle to comprehend.

You're also busy trusting that your Architect is almighty, and that He stays in control of everything, even when it doesn't seem like it. You're not only referring to your own surroundings. It's a challenge to learn what you have control over, and what you need to leave in your Architect's hand. It's extremely difficult to let go and trust God. You don't always understand. Shall you dare to confess that *most* of the times, you actually don't understand. For His ways and His thoughts are so much higher than yours (Isaiah 55:8–9), and you have learned how much it hurts to crash into the wrong border walls.

Your Architect promises that He is in control of the whole process, and that He will make all things work together for good for those who love Him, and is called according to His purpose (Romans 8:28). That is why, even if you feel disheartened as you stare at all the chaos around you, and marvel at how your fellow builders' building and breaking differ from your own, you have to accept and trust that God is busy with them in their own process. As it's written, there's a time for everything—also *"a time to tear down and a time to build"* (Ecclesiastes 3:3, NLT)

As the distractions and oppositions from the outside increase, your level of focus needs to as well. You need to build and keep guard at the same time. Those who don't share in your Building Team's vision, are constantly ready to challenge and attack your plans and progress. The enemy is always near, ready to break down what has been built, to cause confusion, and to move your attention away from your purpose.

Those building accurately, around you and together with you, motivate and encourage you to never give up. You're in the same team and can remind each other to use the right building equipment and gear. You can also sound the trumpet so to speak, make alarm, and warn each other when danger is near.

Also remember, everyone receives the same grace. Live in love as you help each other out and build each other up. When one builder gets extremely tired and needs rest, another can keep guard. Just like Nehemiah appointed groups to build and groups to keep guard (Nehemiah 4:16), there are times when you can rest while others pray, guard, and intercede on your behalf. There will be times when the roles will reverse. There will be times or seasons that you are in a spiritually stronger condition, able to encourage and intercede for others. It's a command from your Architect to carry each other's burdens (Galatians 6:2).

You're starting to grasp the function and purpose of this community, and even beginning to appreciate this whole system. You are also beginning to realise that this is part of God's building plan, the Christ Plan, to function in such unity that no one feels alone, exposed, or helpless. And so, you're starting to understand how the body of Christ fits into the greater building plan.

Just when you get tired of helping out your neighbour repetitively, you also, unexpectedly, experience difficult times. These are humbling experiences, reminding you of the weaknesses in all human beings and increasing your ability to truly empathise. Everyone is in a battle. We weren't promised comfortable lives. To the contrary, to build different than the rest of the world around you, requires bravery. To achieve this in unity, requires discipline and many sacrifices. Nothing about this building process is easy, but your Building Team makes it possible and more than worth it!

It's difficult to carry this responsibility, to build the right way, and at the same time also look out for your fellow builders.

Your natural fleshly building plan constantly has to be brought in line with God's building plan, His righteous plumb line. Constant friction is taking place between these plans.

We are constantly being refined and realigned.

To let go of our own ideas and building plan in exchange for God's, is part of the cross we have to pick up daily. Not only is your sinful, natural plan, going to make things difficult for you, other builders' natural plans are also going to influence and confuse you. Because they're still busy building according to their natural plan; they simply won't understand your new plan. They also won't like your building, because it clashes with so many of their own ideas and beliefs. Constant conversations with your Architect are essential to stay on the right course.

You've had to pack many stones over again. If it wasn't for the grace of your Building Team, you don't know where you would've found the courage to build again after every mistake. Some mistakes are even the same ones—over and over again.

Every time you get discouraged, and want to give up, the Holy Spirit reminds you to check if you have the right gear on, the right building tool in the one hand, and the right weapon in the other.

Discipleship is a constant training process. It requires practice.

The Holy Spirit—Who builds in, through, and with you—provides guidance, teaching, comfort, encouragement, and truth, every moment of every day. You have to focus and tune your ears in to hear His instructions above all the construction noise. He grieves with you every time you refuse to listen or choose to ignore Him. Remember, He is the One handing you all the right gear. Every item is handed over with an explanation of its function, and He trains you to use each tool optimally.

Ephesians 6:10–18 (NLT): "A final word: Be strong in the Lord and in his mighty power. Put on all of God's armour so that you will be able to stand firm against all strategies of the devil. For we are not fighting against flesh-and-blood enemies, but against evil rulers and authorities of the unseen world, against mighty powers in this dark world, and against evil spirits in the heavenly places. Therefore, put on every piece of God's armour so you will be able to resist the enemy in the time of evil. Then after the battle you will still be standing firm. Stand your ground, putting on the belt of truth and the body armour of God's righteousness. For shoes, put on the peace that comes from the Good News so that you will be fully prepared. In addition to all of these, hold up the shield of faith to stop the fiery arrows of the devil. Put on salvation as your helmet, and take the sword of the Spirit, which is the word of God. Pray in the Spirit at all times and on every occasion. Stay alert and be persistent in your prayers for all believers everywhere."

The following building gear-armour needs to be put on daily and intentionally:

The tool belt of truth:

Tighten the tool belt of truth around your middle. The whole outfit is being held together by the belt. All the tools you need are available and easily accessible, enabling you to perform all the necessary functions. All of the instructions are founded in truth, and all of the tools inside the belt testify about the truth. It testifies about the type of building actions that needs to take place. It displays everything your Building Team has told and taught you. There's no room for a lie in this tool belt. To use these tools according to the truth, also highlights the truth for other builders. There can be no dishonesty in your building process. The enemy, the father of lies (John 8:44), really wants to rip this belt of truth off of you because without the truth holding everything together, you're not able to use the rest of your construction clothing. Hold on tightly to the Christ Plan tucked inside your belt of truth, your most valuable item. Study His Architectural Drawing, the blueprint of Christ, before taking any actions.

The reflector vest as the breastplate of righteousness:

The breast plate of righteousness protects your heart from any attacks from the enemy. The Christ Plan that you are built into, provides you with this righteousness. Christ is in you and you are in Christ (John 14:20). Your heart is safe. Your life is safe. Your spirit is safe. When God, your Architect, looks at you, He only sees the building plan of Christ.

His everlasting covenant covers you completely by the blueprint of Christ.

He looks beyond your natural sinful plan and all the mess it has created. He has the vision. He has control. He knows who you are in Him and who He has created you to be. No matter what your emotions are trying to convince you of, and despite all of the lies that are thrown at you to confuse you about your new identity in Christ, God knows you are already sketched into the building plan of Christ.

The Holy Spirit is already busy constructing you into the Christ Plan. It doesn't matter how many mistakes are being made in the process, and how many times you have to break and build up again, God sees the Christ Plan—not the mistakes. Nothing you do or did, could destroy the Christ Plan. Nothing you do or did, could earn your salvation. No good deed could ever make you righteous before God. It's by faith alone that you are saved and this is by pure grace from God (Ephesians 2:8).

This breastplate also has a reflecting function, as all other safety vests on construction sites are required to have. *When God looks at you, Christ is reflected back.* Jesus Christ paid the price and defeated death—He safeguarded your living structure to be fully reconstructed and everlasting!

The safety boots of peace:

As you know and have experienced, you are walking daily on uneven terrain around your construction site. There are many hindrances and obstacles everywhere. To ensure that you work and walk safely, you need to put on the safety boots of the gospel of peace. No matter where you move, always be prepared to tell anyone about God's amazing plan to save and restore humanity. We have the privilege of sharing the good news with other builders that they are also called to build and be built according to the Christ Plan. The *footprints* that you leave testify about the impact that the Christ Plan has had on your own life.

The shield of faith—your plasterboard:

When the construction dust swirls around you, and the enemy tries to attack, just lift up you shield of faith! While you are building, your plasterboard serves two functions: for mixing and moulding the faith that are plastered onto your walls, and also to be a strong and steady shield against any attack.

Every time the enemy attacks you with the lie that your life is still a big rubble mess, and that it would just be better for you to step away from the property, you have to hold on tighter to your plasterboard of faith. You need to keep on building and smoothing out your walls with even more determination! Lift up your plasterboard of faith in front of you—so his accusations and temptations can't penetrate your heart and thoughts.

See how the enemy felt threatened, and mocked the Jews for their faith and efforts in Nehemiah 4:1–2 (NLT) "Sanballat was very angry when he learned that we were *rebuilding* the wall. He flew into a *rage* and *mocked* the Jews, saying in front of his friends and the Samarian army officers, "What does this bunch of poor, feeble Jews think they're doing? Do they really think they can build the wall in a single day by just offering a few sacrifices?" I want to emphasize this part of the second verse in Nehemiah 4:2 (NLT): "*Do they actually think they can make something of stones from a rubbish heap—and charred ones at that?*"

This feels like a familiar line that the enemy throws at believers. He hurls it at us through our own thoughts but also through the words of other people: "Do you *really think* that you can change? Do you *actually think* you can fix this *huge mess*? Do you really think you are *able*? Do you really think these *ruins* can be rebuilt? Do you really think you can be a *new person*? Look at what you're working with! Just give up, you poor fool!"

Hold on to what you believe. Hold on to what the Holy Spirit is teaching you. Hold on *tight* to the promises of God in His Word and to His instructions. Hold on tightly to the truth of your salvation through Christ! The real truth is—you are *not* the one who needs to able to fix the mess—Christ is! Don't allow the enemy to confuse, mislead, distract, or shame you! Stand firm! Lift up your shield of faith!

The hardhat of salvation:

The hardhat protects your mind and thoughts. Everything in God's Word is kept safe and secure in your mind. Your faith is protected. Your hope is secure. When a piece of another builder's wall, or even your own, comes crashing down on you, the hardhat ensures that your faith doesn't get damaged or destroyed. Nothing can take away your salvation in Jesus Christ. Nothing can make God's plan undone. Nothing can take away your Architect's vision and perfect plan. Nothing can stop it. The enemy can't rip up the Christ Plan! You *know* you are saved and stay saved no matter what! The hardhat of salvation serves to remind you over and over again about your salvation, and that you are a new person in Christ (2 Corinthians 5:17).

Your sword as the building trowel—the Word of God:

The most common and useful building equipment is a trowel. A trowel is used to mix, scoop up, and apply cement to buildings. Walls are smoothed out by it, and the handle is also used to tap bricks or stones closer together. *God's Word is also the most important tool to keep in hand during this building process on earth.* Just like Jesus used the Word to battle against the enemy in the desert, we also have to use God's Word as our weapon. Every time you speak and apply God's Word, you are busy smoothing out God's kingdom walls on earth. Every living stone is firmly pressed together in the truth of God's Word. Every time you think about and memorise Scripture, you are busy sharpening your trowel. Just like in the days of Nehemiah, you can't afford to lay down your weapon or building tool. You will need to stay on guard—with the weapon of God's Word in one hand, while you build with the other (Nehemiah 4:17).

There's another very important weapon we seem to miss as we read about the armour of God. Just in the next verse prayer is mentioned as part of the armour. Ephesians 6:18 (NLT): "Pray in the Spirit at all times and on every occasion. Stay alert and be persistent in your prayers for all believers everywhere."

We are not only armoured for our own protection, but to protect other believers as well! And, we use our entire armour prayerfully. *Prayer is the battle strategy for every member of Christ's body and forms part of the entire body's language and communication.*

Never underestimate the power of prayer! James 5:16 (NLT): "The earnest prayer of a righteous person has great power and produces wonderful results." In prayer, we admit to God that we can achieve nothing out of our own strength, we empty and humble our hearts before Him, and ask Him to fight our battles for us—within His will and time. Exodus 14:14 (NLT): "The Lord himself will fight for you. Just stay calm."

Nehemiah also said: "When you hear the blast of the trumpet, rush to wherever it's sounding. Then our God will fight for us!" (Nehemiah 4:17, NLT).

Take careful notice of how Nehemiah's battle to reconstruct Jerusalem's walls, started *and* ended with prayer (Nehemiah 1:4 and 13:31). Although Nehemiah physically had to plan and move, his spirit was always focused on God. He approached the entire challenge prayerfully. Before he took any actions, he first prayed to God for help, provision, and guidance. He even prayed throughout the whole project before taking any actions (Nehemiah 2:4). The whole wall was repaired in just 52 weeks (Nehemiah 6:15) because of God's favor that rested on Nehemiah. That is the power of prayer!

All of our construction work ought to start and end in prayer.

Be assured, that for as long as you live, the building dust will be blowing and blazing around you! But be assured, that you are equipped to end the battle as more than a conqueror! Lift up your building tool, lift up your weapon, and press on! Even though you get tired, you won't fall. And if you stumble, you won't stay down. Even when your flesh gets tired and tender, your spirit stays strong and safe! You can do anything through Christ, who gives you strength (Philippians 4:13).

My building War Cry

Knees bent, prayerfully preparing
Then, confidently rising
Picking up both tool and sword,
Knowing the battle belongs to the Lord
Newly clothed and fully equipped
To simultaneously protect and build
Your kingdom walls
Within and around me –
Creating and contributing to unity
Filled with Your wisdom and Your Spirit
To implement strategies of outstanding merit
Gloriously geared for Your purpose –
Preparing the way and smoothing the surface
To reflect walls
Built righteously and straight
And positioning guards at the gates
Fully aware –
Resting and resisting,
Watching and building,
One stone at a time, I persevere
Encouraging fellow builders that are near,
About the full-blown victory
When the capstone will be placed
All our efforts rewarded and weighed,
We've not a moment to waste!
Amen.

Chapter 8

Labour: Work-Rest Balance in God

God's promise of entering his rest still stands, *so we ought to tremble with fear that some of you might fail to experience it.*
—Hebrews 4:1 (NLT)

The building labour is hard and unceasing. In the natural building world, there's a well-known joke about understanding the three parts of building—it always takes three times as long, costs twice as much as planned, and you're only willing to do it once. Any construction project involves frustration and hindrances. The costs are high, and no one ever says they're happy about making a mistake. Physically and emotionally, it costs you. It really requires perseverance.

The construction will require the willingness to adjust your agenda to fit the process, but never give up on the entire process. You always need to keep the end product in mind and stay focused on the goal.

There are times you get to rest and catch your breath, but your mind never shuts down. This building process throughout life never ends. You never forget about God's vision or your responsibilities. You never forget about the building plan or its progress. It's with an expectant and hopeful heart that you wait for that day when your building will be completed! Every day involves the persistence and labour needed to continue building so you can reach the end in victoriously. Wise choices and disciplined actions are essential to get sufficient rest throughout the process.

The realisation is sinking in deeper and deeper, that this building which you are constructing with and through the Holy Spirit, is part of you. Not only do you live in this building, but you *are* the building that is being built according to the Christ Plan. On Him, in Him, with Him, you are being sanctified and rebuilt. The discipleship process is the style or technique according to which you are rebuilt into His righteousness.

The building you are being built into, is connected to all the other buildings around you through relationships. Everyone is being built up by the Holy Spirit in unity. He unifies our hearts, desires, vision, purpose and minds. Everybody works hard. Everybody craves rest.

There is only one true Spirit, the Holy Spirit, Who follows our God, the Architect's, instructions. There is only one way of building and one truth. There is only one plan and specific Cornerstone. There can be no division in this building, otherwise we are busy building against God's plan and against the work of the Holy Spirit (Luke 11:23). Because the same Spirit that is living in you, is also living in your fellow builders, you are forming part of a greater unity and spiritual family. Everyone is fulfilling their function to benefit the entire body of Christ. According to 1 Peter 4:10 we need to serve one another with our gifts. The gifts are given to be shared.

The body of Christ, is like a great temple building containing every believer-building, each contributing to the reinforcement, wholeness, and function of the entire temple.

Your building touches those closest to you first—your spouse, children, grandchildren, parents, other family members, and friends of faith. Furthermore, your building contributes to society's unity and strength, as the whole building is constructed in Him. Every building not built according to the Christ Plan, is like an unstable obstacle in the way of God's perfect plan. By being the light and the salt of the earth (Matthew 5:13–16), our lives serve as an example of building righteously.

Your whole life, you're entire building, is a visible testimony of everlasting sustainability.

Because you yourself *are* the living, breathing, building, the building process can never come to a standstill. Work and rest are such complicated concepts for us to understand because it's not only applicable to our physical being. Every moment that your heart beats and your lungs draw breath, you are physically working. Even when you are unconscious, you are still working while you are resting. Everyone of us are constantly busy serving other people with our time and abilities, so the whole body of Christ is also always working. Even Solomon encourages us to watch how ants work and learn from them (Proverbs 6:6).

The work on your soul and spirit also never comes to a halt. Paul says that we are *constantly busy being transformed* into the image of the Lord, receiving this glory, that is Spirit, from Him (2 Corinthians 3:18). How do we truly enter rest then? We know we have to physically rest. Without it we would burn out and even die from exhaustion. But how do our souls and spirits rest within this spiritual building process?

God, our Architect, has given us His entire Word full of instructions, revelations, and wisdom to help us practice and achieve this work-rest balance in Him. The Holy Spirit not only guides you to take actions, but to find rest in God, and in what He has done through Christ. There are no other sources of rest in this spiritual building process.

Just like a builder takes his lunch and tea breaks on this physical earth, we also have to take precious "breaks" throughout this spiritual labour. Nehemiah understood the value of rest and how much the builders needed it. That's why he divided the people in groups, so some could keep guard, while others rested (Nehemiah 4:21–22). Because God is our Source and has everything under His control, we find rest and replenishment in His presence.

It's extremely difficult to hear His voice above the construction noise. You will need to intentionally enter your inner room, close the door and pray to your heavenly Father (Matthew 6:6).

God invites us to be still and know that He is God (Psalm 46:10). When we get overwhelmed and the building dust is flying—with our energy levels low and frustration levels high—we have to force ourselves to become still and focus on God. We need to listen to His voice, His plan, His promises, and His instructions. We need to let go of unnecessary burdens, and stretch out our tired empty hands so He can fill us continuously with His Spirit and His strength.

It's during these quiet moments that God looks at our wounds and take care of them, that the Holy Spirit clears the dust and sweeps away the cob webs, filling our entire capacity with His light and love, moving around the furniture of our lives so our priorities line up again with His.

It's in the quiet moments that we reflect on the beauty and wonder of the Christ Plan—so complicated, yet so simple—a genius work of God. Even during the times that we struggle to hear God's voice, and battle to stay aware of the Holy Spirit's presence, God invites us to trust Him. Trust that He is who He says He is, trust that He is almighty and in control, trust in His timing, and trust in His plan. In the difficult quiet moments when we sense the resistance of the enemy increasing, while we guard and build, we find our rest in knowing that God is God. No matter what He says or allows or what your emotions are signalling to you—you're spirit rests in God, Who is Spirit (John 4:24).

We find rest in knowing that we don't need to understand or defend God. We find rest in trusting His ways. Proverbs 3:5–6 (NLT): "Trust in the Lord with all your heart, do not depend on your own understanding. Seek His will in all you do, and He will show you which path to take." We find rest by handing our worries over to Him (1 Peter 5:7). Jesus asks us to come to Him to receive rest for our souls—His yoke is easy and His burden is light (Matthew 11:28–30).

Even though it takes work to be built into Christ's image, it's a lighter load and simpler process than the chaotic one the world provides.

There will be a very distinct difference in the labour of those who build their lives according to the Christ Plan, and those who build according to worldly ambitions. There will be a very clear difference in the way the groups rest and recharge. *When you construct your building according to worldly standards, there will be little rest for your soul. Psalm 127:1 (NLT): "Unless the Lord builds a house, the work of the builders is wasted."*

Those that build according to the worldly style and expectations, struggle to find rest because they are constantly trying to achieve success and maintain an image for other builders to admire. Pride motivates and keeps them moving. They find their value in achievements and their security in financial means. Those who haven't found their image in Christ, are constantly driven to find and create their own identity. They are constantly searching for a way to add *value* and some type of *meaning* to their existence. When they don't want to receive their restoration from God—their salvation from Christ—they turn to worldly sources for comfort and company.

Habits, addictions, and unhealthy relationships develop, that won't ever be able to fulfil what they're soul is truly craving for. It's extremely exhausting work when it all comes down to yourself.

The builders that have accepted the Christ Plan, know that there's nothing they could ever do to make themselves righteous, whole or perfect. They know that Jesus paid the price in full with His blood and that their value lies in Him. Only faith makes it possible to build on this Christ Plan, and even faith comes not from ourselves, but is a gift from God. They hold on to Ephesians 2:8–10 (NLT): "For it's by grace you have been saved, through faith—and this is not from yourselves, it's a gift of God—not by works, so that no one can boast."

They know it's all grace. Pure grace is their resting place

Gordon Neufeld, a developmental psychologist whose work focuses on attachment between parents and their children, said the following: *"Children must never work for our love, they must rest in it."* How powerful is that statement when we apply it to our relationship with our heavenly Father! It helps us to understand what this rest in God really means—we don't have to work for His love or provision, we were meant to *rest in His love.*

When you build according to God's plan, there will be rest for your soul and peace that surpasses human understanding. As your faith grows, there will be no place for fear, for He fills your building with His Spirit of power, love, and self-control (2 Timothy 1:7). Even when you don't understand everything, life will still make sense to you.

You will find rest in knowing that God has a plan for your life, that He knows you, has called you, has saved you through Christ, sealed you with the Holy Spirit, and is working in and through you, every living moment. You will find rest in knowing your reward and crown is waiting for you in heaven (Matthew 5:10–12). It might even happen before then, when Christ returns (Revelation 22:12). Until then, we rest in His promises and that is why the peace that Christ gives, is different from the peace, or rather *lack of peace*, that the world provides (John 14:27).

We know that if we only rested, nothing would ever be done. As important as it is to rest for our physical and spiritual rejuvenation, it's equally important to work for God and through His Holy Spirit. And when we pick up our building equipment, let's do it wholeheartedly and with passion! Work and rest are both important powerful elements in the construction of this spiritual building, but there has to be a *balance.* We need to be continually filled with the rivers of the Holy Spirit to achieve this. The disciples were being filled with the Holy Spirit and with joy

(Acts 13:52). It's written in the *present tense*. *Being filled* with the Holy Spirit is not a once-off occasion, it's a *continuous process*. A river never stops flowing, other wise it would turn into a lake. The Holy Spirit flows like a river!

Not only did God provide the building plan and revealed His mysterious plan to you, He also sent the Holy Spirit to guide and supervise the building process, while also strengthening you and providing everything necessary to complete this project. Don't listen to your flesh when you feel tired and frustrated. Look beyond the physical struggles and see the victory in the spirit! This is where your true rest lies. Be at peace in believing that your foundation is steady. You don't have to go through life off balance and feeling it's all meaningless. When you face pain and all different kinds of challenges in life, remind yourself that this life is only temporary (1 Chronicles 29:15).

Find your peace in the fact that you will never fit into the worldly building design, and that you were never meant to. Your building is supposed to look different. Your eyes are always looking up and forward. Don't allow your focus to settle on the hardships you're busy facing. Your faith is being refined like precious gold, and God is busy shaping your character structure, perfecting it little by little, moment to moment (1 Peter 1:7).

Physically, rest is possible for your body. Psalm 3:5 (NLT): "I lay down and slept, yet I woke up in safety, for the Lord was watching over me." However, there are times that we struggle to find rest. Even Paul battled with a thorn in his flesh that God chose not to remove (2 Corinthians 12:7). But even then, we find rest in God's promise that He makes all things work together for our good and for His glory (Romans 8:28). So even when you don't always experience the physical rest you so desperately crave for, your thoughts, and soul, can safely rest in God. Whether it's going good or bad—you know you can trust that God is in control and that He knows where He is directing your very steps.

Declare with David the following from Psalm 62:6–8 (NLT):

"He alone is my rock and my salvation, my fortress where I will not be shaken. My victory and honor come from God alone. He is my refuge, a rock where no enemy can reach me. O my people, trust in Him at all times. Pour out your heart to Him, for God is our refuge."

Don't get tired of pressing on and doing these good works. Galatians 6:9 (NLT) "So let's not get tired of doing what is good. At just the right time we will reap a harvest of blessing if we don't give up." Let's continue building with passion, until the day that we will enter eternal rest!

I Will Rest and Rejoice in You

What does this "rest" mean, Lord?
For I never stop labouring, breathing...
Never allow myself to be bored
You're inviting me to lay down on a green hill
To stop, and know, and be still...
To carry a lighter load—working but resting:
Balancing the giving and receiving
In the quiet I know that You are
I realise my superficial control is bizarre
For You created me –
And every other thing
You want me to rest in Your perfection:
The divine plan from the beginning of creation
You never intended for us to struggle
Rest was secure in Eden
You never wanted us to juggle –
So many tasks, so many worldly lies
The resting is found in relationship
Which breaks the yoke and stronghold ties
Your life, and heaven, cannot be earned
A gift of grace, I have learned
My tired soul rejoices
In the promise and hope of total restoration
Already tasting goodness in this spiritual formation
I will rejoice during the trials and refining
Consistently redefining:
The purpose, the pain –
Never in vain
Even in grief I'll rejoice
Making a disciplined choice:
To celebrate Your love, carrying me through
Drawing spiritual strength from this joy found in You!
Amen.

PART 3
FINISHING TOUCHES
AND MAINTENANCE

Chapter 9

Building, Breaking, and Boundaries

*I said to them, "**Do not leave the gates open during the hottest part of the day**. And even while **the gatekeepers** are on **duty**, have them shut and bar the doors. **Appoint the residents** of Jerusalem **to act as guards**, everyone on a **regular watch**. Some will **serve** at sentry posts and some in front of their **own homes**.*
—Nehemiah 7:3 (NLT)

The clear lines of Christ, the Cornerstone, are becoming more visible and prominent in the construction of your spiritual building. As the building process progresses, you realise that these lines do not only serve as guidelines, but also as *boundaries*.

Colossians 2:6–7 (NLT): "And now, just as you accepted Christ Jesus as your Lord, you must continue to follow Him. Let your roots grow down into Him, and let your lives be built on him. Then your faith will grow strong in the truth you were taught, and you will overflow with thankfulness."

As you are being built on the Christ Plan, all the necessary boundaries are becoming more evident. You're also learning that boundaries are there for your good and His glory. God is not trying to limit your needs or restrict your unique expressions, but rather encouraging you to pursue and fulfil it all in the fullness of the Christ Plan. Building on the Christ Plan leads to a life of abundance! (John 10:10) The boundaries of the Christ Plan are equal to your new identity, life style, and building style, as a disciple of Jesus Christ. It's part of the instructions from your heavenly Architect.

The Holy Spirit continues to teach you about ownership—God's, as well as your own.

Boundary lines indicate where property starts and ends. The rights and responsibilities of the owner of the property fall within the boundary lines. Boundaries not only serve as a sign of restricted access to outsiders but especially protect what is being kept within. In the same way it's our Architect's will that boundaries are built around and within our spiritual building—to keep away that which shouldn't form part of your building but also to protect what is being built for Him.

Rather than viewing boundaries as legalistic and unrealistic restrictive rules, we can look at them as holy strategies and instructions to protect the work God is doing within and through us.

Boundaries are not instructions for now and then, it's a whole life style. God's instructions and boundaries ensure the safety of your soul and your inner peace. That is why there's so much joy and freedom to enjoy within these sanctifying boundaries! It protects our purpose, and promotes our construction for His glory! It advances the expansion of God's kingdom on earth, and enhances our taste of heaven!

It's when we cross the boundaries that we feel the consequences on our own living stones. That's when we experience our greatest vulnerability and open ourselves up for damage. We feel guilty when we build the wrong way and choose shortcut techniques. We sense the way we are grieving the Holy Spirit when we intentionally build against His supervising instruction. Shame overwhelms us easily when our stones come tumbling down in the presence of God. We feel tired and hopeless when we try to build out of our own strength and forget that we'll only accomplish this great work through the strength of God's Spirit (Zachariah 4:6).

We get hurt when wrong stones are thrown at others, and also thrown back at us. The Holy Spirit makes us so aware when we are not acting or reacting according to His loving guidance. An awake conscience forms part of the package deal from the day you decide to build upon the Christ Plan. Sometimes, we make only one wrong decision and a whole wall comes crashing down! To top it all off, it might be the specific wall that you've really worked on the hardest and for the longest time. When we step away from the Holy Spirit's guidance, we easily bump and rub against another person's living stones in the wrong way.

Boundaries not only protect our own building process, but also the people close to us. We also mustn't forget about the little buildings in our lives that are watching our building style and constructing according to our example.

As the Holy Spirit helps us to build in line with God's plan for our lives, we learn so many new things. One of those things are setting the right boundaries. We learn when to say yes, and when to say no. Because we are actively building together with the Holy Spirit, it requires self-control and disciplined actions from our own side. We are not alone, but we can't just stand back and do nothing. Every day we'll experience the temptation to follow the old, easier, and more familiar building plan that makes more sense to us in physical terms. The natural plan which provides so much satisfaction in the here and now because it's visibly clear, tangible, and can be experienced immediately through your senses, thoughts, and emotions. There will also be an ongoing battle with the honour you desire—from people or from God.

Every day we face the choice to lay down the sinful desires of the flesh—carnal desires that are not building us up in a godly and glorifying way. That is why prayer and fasting are such powerful construction tools to help us build on the right plan. We not only fast for specific matters during specific times, we actually fast daily from the things and building techniques—the sinful stones—that are damaging and delaying the construction of our spiritual building.

It's a sanctifying process—being built upon and into Christ. Little by little, every moment, we are being built and refined into His image. We are all able to notice the buildings that are being restored and built up through this sanctifying process, to be a light and a beacon of hope to those around them. Those buildings that have radically changed from building according to the worldly plan to building according to the Christ Plan, reflecting something of God's glory and His amazing restorative power. Their lives are testimonies of hope.

We see in front of our very eyes the real transformation as broken rubble heaps are restored into whole and stabile buildings. We see those once broken-down buildings reaching out with their livings stones towards other broken buildings, encouraging them to also follow the Christ Plan. It's the only plan leading to true wholeness, in the present moment, but especially in the future. Living, whole walls, that are reaching out and providing support to those that are unstable, those busy building up their strength. Living stones that are shining out love and light to unmask and expel the darkness and cold around them. Those living buildings that have been so radically transformed, have often conquered their own fears with His truth, and want to encourage others to also take this leap of faith.

It's extremely challenging and uncomfortable to break down your only standing walls for something different and unfamiliar. All of us need support. No one has to complete this difficult process all by themselves. The enemy will often lie and try to convince you that you're all alone and won't ever be understood. *The enemy breaks unity. But the Holy Spirit unifies and connects the believer-buildings.*

Look around you, there are so many reinforced buildings available close by that truly wants to support and assist you. None of them are perfect. They are also going through the same type of things you are. Some you will find in a church setting, some in a support group or a social group. Maybe it's that one that invited you for coffee or an outing or the one that noticed you were having a really tough day. Our God is faithful—He'll never let you be alone. It's His will and part of His plan that there will always be people blessed with the Holy Spirit's fruit and gifts, serving one another and functioning as one body. He knows what you need.

This construction process will never work or be successful in isolation. Fear will only hold you back. As highlighted before, God didn't give us a spirit of fear, but of power, love, and self-control (2 Timothy 1:7). This power, love, and self-control indicates specifics and boundaries. The stones that are daily built into your spiritual building that oppose these three boundaries, need to be removed. God is merciful and always forgive our sins. It's just a pity that they damage our own and other people's buildings. It wastes so much time that could've been used to build for His glory. It's time-consuming and painful to lay the wrong stones and set them in concrete, just to break them out and build again.

God's grace allows us to see every mistake we make, to rectify it and build again in line with our Cornerstone. It's His will to grant us this grace and opportunities. He never violates our boundaries when we make decisions. If God is the Creator of everything, He must also be the Creator of boundaries—*good boundaries*. And since everything is held together by Christ (Colossians 1:17), we find all we need to understand these boundaries, in Christ. With the power and loving guidance of the Holy Spirit, we apply our self-control to build this life and His Spirit's dwelling place for and with Him. The more you understand God's plan, the more humbled, honoured, loved, and willing you'll be to let go of your own plans for His!

It's part of our earthly existence and temporary battle to stand strong against the vision of the natural building plan. Paul explains how he can't comprehend why he does what he doesn't want to do and don't do the things he wants to do in Roman 7:15–20. This is a man that has had a powerful experience and meeting with Jesus Christ on the road to Damascus, and who's life has been radically changed to glorify God. But he was still a normal human being, exposed to the elements, and his own fleshly desires. The sanctifying process requires your self-disciplined participation. The Holy Spirit doesn't take over and control your actions, He changes you from the inside out. When we are obedient the change takes place faster and become more prominent—it's the visible fruit of the Holy Spirit.

We literally see and experience the renovations of our spiritual building taking on shape, form, and beauty. When we resist and choose to be disobedient, the renovation takes much longer.

Paul also described his frustration about a thorn in His flesh that God chose not to remove, even though he prayed for deliverance from this struggle (2 Corinthians 12:7). Paul had a very real, normal struggle. This great man, who had been called by Jesus Christ to proclaim the good news of salvation to the gentiles, who wrote most of the New Testament letters, risked his life for the gospel, planted and guided churches—and all this while being a mentor and spiritual leader to many other believers. One would expect that God's favor would ensure an easier journey and more blessings along the way—more open doors, not closed ones. But if you study Paul's life, you'll see a very different picture, one most of us would not want to trade for our own. Shipwrecked, imprisoned, alone and isolated for long periods of time, and eventually killed for his faith. He was obedient to Christ's calling, even though he didn't receive all the blessings or answers he desperately craved for. But he trusted God. He learned through his suffering that Christ's strength is sufficient to accomplish what he was called to do and that God's grace is sufficient for his needs. It kept him humble. It kept him begging for more grace and strength! *It kept him close to God.*

It's our physical and spiritual battles that keep us humbly tuned into God's plan. Sometimes those battles are part of the boundaries that are preventing us from following our own natural ideas. Maybe they're valuable boundaries, protecting us and preventing us from building out of the lines.

As long as we are living and breathing on this earth, we will be imperfect human beings, fighting the good fight till the bitter end. Even when we're changed, the world isn't changed for us. Temptations and hard-hearted people aren't removed. We are exposed to all the darkness and brokenness of other human beings, and the consequences of their actions—which we can't control. God let's the sun shine over good and bad people (Matthew 5:45).

Just as other people's darkness affects us, the light of Christ within us also has an effect on them.

That's why we must never lose hope or give up. Things won't always make sense if we try to understand it from our limited human reasoning. We need to have grace for ourselves and each other in this process. It's the only way to learn that God's strength reaches its full capacity within us when we are at our weakest. It's how we realise that we desperately need Him, and accept the truth that we don't know how to build this spiritual building on our own. Draw near to God and He will draw near to you (James 4:8). It's within this relationship and unity with God, Jesus Christ, and Holy Spirit, that we can build with a confident hope.

There'll be days when you look back in wonder and awe at what has been constructed during a time that you experienced as chaotic and challenging. Sometimes, we only see the truly amazing transformation that has taken place when we step back, away from all the construction dust.

At times we are so blinded and confused that we don't even realise we're still busy building—breaking down wrong walls and faulty stones are so important for us to be able to build the new walls. We don't always realise that we create a lot of extra work for ourselves. With our fallen nature, we're going to build and demolish many wrong walls. Even though we strive with all our might to do the right things all the time, it's an impossible task. If it was possible, we'd never need saving, and grace would lose its powerful purpose. Even though your spiritual building shows progress and you can see the spiritual growth and fruit in your life, the Holy Spirit will always keep you aware of God's grace.

As our buildings mature, we become wiser, and learn how to stop building the wrong walls sooner. When we follow His instructions, when we wait on the Lord, and when we actively participate in the work of the Holy Spirit, the amount of sinful stones that need to be removed become less. *Our spiritual arms become stronger and capable of picking up and placing the right stones in the right places. We receive wisdom and discernment to make better choices in the future.*

That is why God teaches us the wonder of boundaries. Boundaries come in various forms and are connected to *guarding*. We are instructed to place a guard in front of our mouths (Proverbs 13:3) and our hearts (Proverbs 4:23). We'll find God's Word full of boundaries—what is right and wrong. There are many stories, parables, examples, and advice to help and guide us to say yes to the right things, and say no to the wrong things.

This spiritual building that we are being built into isn't static, it's living! It moves and has impact. We are *living* stones! It's like we have an opening that connects us to God. We need to be filled with the Holy Spirit *continuously* (Acts 13:52). It's an instruction for all believers throughout the discipleship process. Without the filling of the Holy Spirit, we are dark, dead, static buildings. But the Holy Spirit breathes life into our dead stones and fill us with the light of Christ! And then He wants us to display His light to all that are still stuck in darkness (Mark 4:21-34).

We are also not solid, isolated structures. *Together,* we form the living stones of the greater spiritual house that is being built for God's Spirit (1 Peter 2:5–9). It's like we also have an opening that allows us to reach out and connect to each other as the body parts of Christ, fulfilling our unique functions as we serve one another and live as a unit.

As the Scripture from Nehemiah in the beginning of this

chapter explains, we need to be awake and alert. Of course, we need gates and openings—through them we live, communicate, receive, and give. Our physical survival depends on it. In the same way, our spiritual body and the greater body of Christ also depend on it. We need to reach out to one another to offer help, support, and encouragement in times of sorrow. We also need to reach out to one another to rejoice and celebrate together in times filled with joy and goodness. We are meant to do it all together. But having these gates and openings, also leaves us extremely *vulnerable*.

We don't just need boundaries to contain and define this body of believers' purpose, we especially need openings, and along with it guards that protect these openings. The Holy Spirit in each of us, flows through our united body as we receive and share His gifts. That is why we should appreciate each other's gifts and not be envious—the gifts do not belong to one member only, but to all believers, to the entire body of Christ.

The gifts of the Holy Spirit only become real gifts when we share them. If someone has the gift to encourage others in their faith but keep it to themselves, the gift loses its value. It stays hidden and passive within that body member, and then none can share in its blessing and purpose. You see, if one misses out, we all miss out, and when one receives and shares, we all receive and are blessed! Because we are living stones, connected to one another, touching each other's lives, we need guards in front of our hearts and mouths to ensure what flows through our body is good and God-glorifying.

We need to take each thought captive and make it obedient to Christ (2 Corinthians 10:5). Any idea or plan that doesn't align with the Christ Plan, needs to be rejected and not entertained as a guest within the body. It pollutes your entire building. What's going on in your thoughts and heart on the inside, affects what you let out. We are known by our fruit and our root lies deep within the middle of our structure—inside our hearts. Bitterness, hate, jealousy, and everything that isn't from the Holy Spirit, need to be removed and kept outside the boundaries. You are ultimately responsible to keep guard in front of these boundaries. You are responsible for the things leaking out of your own building and which are also affecting your neighbours. Earlier in the book we looked at cells within the body of Christ that become like cancer cells. We need to protect the body of Christ against this and all other spiritual diseases.

We build and break as He leads us. We persevere and press forward, our vision broadens, focused on His kingdom, focused and our purpose. Lines need to be drawn and guarded to build His kingdom. At times we will need to stand guard in front of certain openings to protect the people close to our hearts. Parents guard the openings to their homes and also their children's hearts. Parents and care givers not only construct their own spiritual buildings according to God's instructions, but serve as examples and guards in the discipleship process of their children's spiritual construction. God placed this right and responsibility for children within parents' domain and boundaries. Proverbs 22:6 (NLT): "Direct your children onto the right path, and when they are older, they will not leave it." Ephesians 6:4 (NLT): "Fathers, do not provoke your children to anger, but bring them up in the discipline and instruction of the Lord."

Husbands and wives need to stand guard, carefully considering what they allow to enter their marriage and what to keep outside. All Scripture about love and relationships are applicable to marriage.

Churches, schools, and communities all have openings requiring guards. In the greater building, the body of Christ, we are responsible for our own actions but also for looking out for each other and to make alarm when an intruder is approaching an opening.

Nehemiah appointed a trumpet blower to make alarm if, and when, the enemy approached the wall. Each one of us need to be informed and understand what are expected from us—where we need to take responsibility with boundaries, and where we need to take a step further and make alarm to protect another building.

Be especially careful to not get deceived into using the old building techniques. Hold on to the truth and the new covenant of the Christ Plan. Remember always, that the Christ Plan was offered to you by and through grace. There's nothing that can be done by works to deserve it. However, when you really grasp the wonder of this opportunity, you will receive the heart's desire to build according to Christ's way.

We understand by now that we have received the construction outfit and gear as armour. We know that we need to put it on daily to build in a successful and safe way. We realise that we're fellow builders in the construction of God's greater kingdom and His Spirit's dwelling place. We also understand that we need to start at our own building, then the buildings around us, and that we all perform a specific and special function within the greater building and body of Christ. We know that we need to learn about our building equipment. We need to prayerfully practise and train to use it in the correct way at the right time. With our weapon in our other hand, we're always ready to resist the enemy. We build and we fight with God's instructions and the power of the Holy Spirit.

We're not cold, empty buildings, but full of light and life through the Holy Spirit living within us. We are sealed by Him (Ephesians 1:13). By staying within the right boundaries and keeping guard over the actions performed through our openings and boundaries, we can prevent unnecessary damage and save the time spent on breaking down wrong walls, and rather spend it on building righteous plumb line walls. There'll always be weak moments when we accidentally overlook a boundary or get deceived by an undercover intruder, but the Holy Spirit will shine His light on the subject and always bring you back in line.

This brings us to the essence of this building contract between you and God—GRACE. Received by grace and maintained by grace. It's only when we are able to receive grace, that we are able to give grace.

Building Boundaries

Your Holy Spirit's light falls and shines
Revealing safe boundaries and divine lines
Within which my soul is rebuilt and restored
Into Your plan and image all the more
Requiring building and breaking,
Assisting this sanctifying shaping
I am learning and partaking
While dead bones are waking
As grace and peace abounds
I always listen for the trumpet sound –
Guarding and protecting,
Rebuilding, and not wrecking
What you have assigned
Consistently transforming my mind
Regulating the function of my soul's doors,
Letting go of my plans for Yours
Supporting nearby structures also
For Your Spirit connects us to grow
Together our living stones are being built
Into Your final temple that will never wilt.
Amen.

Chapter 10

*...My grace is sufficient for you, for my
power is made perfect in weakness...*
—2 Corinthians 12:9 (NIV)

It's been a while that you've been building on the new plan, and it looks like you're displaying progress. You're getting to know your Building Team better each day, and also starting to understand their instructions more clearly. Every now and then, you receive new revelations and a deeper appreciation for the new building style of the Christ Plan.

It remains a challenge, and constantly requires deliberate input from your own side. Some days, disciplined actions are easier to perform than others. At times, you experience a difficult day or even a difficult season, where you question the free choices that you make or the challenging situations that you face. But overall, you feel that you're making good progress in this discipleship process.

From where you are currently standing—looking out of your building—it has become easier to clearly see and discern the way that other people are building. It has also become easier to offer some advice and opinions. Even when you don't always share a somewhat critical opinion out loud, you can't get away from the stormy conversations inside of you.

Mistakes stand out. It's so much easier to notice and point out a flaw than to acknowledge and celebrate a small success. You are convinced people need to know that there's a right and a wrong. At times you're blissfully unaware of the judgemental conversations taking place between your own head and heart. It happens so subtly on a subconscious level. Some things are just so tough to openly admit to other people. It can be even more difficult to admit it to yourself!

There are still dark corners in your building that you haven't seen. That's understandable. Nobody can see what happens in the darkness. You're quite shocked every time another dark corner is exposed. You wonder when that will end. Wonder *if* it will ever end. That's how the sanctification process works. Thus far, you only comprehend what has been brought into the light.

You wish everybody could notice and follow the way that you're building in the light. You honestly believe that you're doing it the right way. You desperately want to help and pass on the light—yes—want to shed some light on somebody else's dark corners and actions.

You're especially proud of a certain straight wall of yours, one that clearly testifies of your obedience and dedication to God's plan. It stands nice and open in the bright light, unashamed.

The thought that God is taking each of His children through a unique process is uncomfortable and not yet fully entertained. Aren't we all part of one greater spiritual building? Then, you reckon and justify, there ought to be some consistency and uniformity. Everyone's input matters, right? Then why don't people follow your advice, steps for success and spiritual growth, when they can clearly see you're getting something right in a certain area?

If you're an extrovert, you try to share this personal message straightforward and to the point within your inner circle or any new willing acquaintances. It's even being shared and demonstrated in a very clear and personal yet quite impersonal way on social media. You're completely oblivious to the fact that you might be seeking some praise and acceptance from people. You do it all for a good cause. The inner room conversations with God are becoming replaced more often with conversations on social media.

It's so convenient, being able to post, edit, and share all your pretty straight walls in public. It's soothing to the soul, to the ego. What is beautiful, is beautiful, right? Good beliefs that are shared easy and wide.

Even the introverts are experiencing the pressure and fear of being left out. They also have it on their hearts to share and make their evangelical contribution on social media. It creates some form of social contact, without it being too intimidating. Perfect! Sometimes you can just pray, worship, or testify from your couch, without everything getting too personal or uncomfortable. Everybody's learning to be content with this virtual type of fellowship. Hopefully, you get a few people and if you're completely honest, any people that like your post and agree with what you're saying. The more likes and shares, the more valuable the message you're getting out there, right? Maybe you'll really help save a soul online, who will ever know? It's not impossible. Some messages are extremely popular, trendy, and your mind automatically starts to move along with the main stream. You wonder why so many people lack the passion to agree with everything that you're sharing, and when they'll start to see that you're promoting the right way. Without realising, our ego's get calmed or hurt, and we start to lose focus of the whole truth of the gospel.

Pride and self-righteousness enter your gates well disguised.

When the focus on ourselves become too intense, we quickly look away. Looking at the painful skew walls of the building next to us, we can only sigh. The whole thing is being constructed in the wrong direction and looks ready to collapse at any second. It's so easy to see all the mistakes from your vantage point from the outside. How much longer is that builder going to be so hard of hearing? Can't they see that they just need to make simple choices for change and then stick with it. They just need the right direction and some self-discipline.

Don't they get the discipleship process? Can't they hear the Holy Spirit's instructions? Do they really understand the Architect's plan? Are they even really saved and building on the Christ Plan? Why do they do what they shouldn't do and don't do what they should? What conversations are taking place within those buildings? It's all very vague and unknown territory to you. They're definitely still caught up in some darkness. Why can't they see all that darkness within? You hope the light breaks through for them, and soon. And if they really don't want to hear or see, then they can just continue on building a mess and suffer the consequences. How many times do they need to be confronted, anyways?

Their building is a real frustrating and disgusting eyesore in your life. It's something you don't even want to look at anymore. You just can't handle having it so close to you, right in front of your view.

That's why you're starting to give more frequent and specific advice, even handing over a neat package of some of the instructions that have worked for you. They have to use their building equipment so and so. Why did they let their weapon fall there? Why didn't they listen for the trumpet sound? Do they still not know their enemy and how to stand guard? Many times, you wish you could just lift up your whole building from the ground, and move it as far away from them—as far away as possible. Then everyone can give each other space and build the way they want.

You're so far along with your building process and your spiritual structure has grown so much. The days of skew walls and building dust are either long forgotten or semi-forgotten. You're busy with different walls at this stadium. You try to block the bad memories that surface. You try to move on. Your subconscious is preventing you to move back to that big sore gap in your past.

Here and there, you notice some broken walls because they look exactly like yours did. Then you *do* have compassion and empathy for the familiar walls. The others, well, that's a different story.

Then there comes a day. And as time goes by, you learn that there will be many more days like that one.

A day that a wall you thought was built perfectly and with immense effort, falls. Hard. Undoubtedly. Painful. Building dust flying as far as your eyes can see...

No, Lord!

What happened now? You honestly thought you were on the right track, building within the right lines. Suddenly, something is off in a relationship with someone that is very significant to you. Suddenly, you see a part of yourself that you really didn't want to see. Suddenly, this wall that came tumbling down, causes a tremendous after shock within your inner core and your structure shakes ferociously. Shaky and angry, you begin to seriously debate with yourself and with your Building Team about what just happened. Oblivious, you even throw in a few accusations towards them. You are completely rattled. It feels unfair.

Then it happens—the Light falls on a dark corner that you couldn't see while you were so busy building upwards and forwards. The Holy Spirit had given gentle warnings along the way that you couldn't or didn't want to hear. You faintly remember it. The wall you were building so successfully, needed to be torn down, otherwise that dark corner would have stayed hidden forever.

As life continues and time goes on, you learn that the Light will fall unexpectedly like that many more times, exposing all the dark areas you fail to notice. As if it's not bad enough to become aware of certain weak places within your building, you also find out that while you wanted to point out and illuminate other people's dark corners, some of them felt exactly the same way towards you.

Here you experience it again—the shame. You wanted to move far away from it and never experience it again. You're a new creation in Christ. What went wrong?

The Holy Spirit's Light moves softly and slowly over the broken pieces of concrete between your stones that have tumbled to the ground. You notice all the cracks in it: bitterness, unforgiveness, comparison, jealousy, ungratefulness, self-justification… the list goes on. What you've always considered to be 'good judgement' in the dark, is undoubtedly exposed as 'pride' within the Light. You still want to defend that *surely* it has to be a good type of pride, but the Light makes it impossible to hide the truth. You honestly meant it so well…

You are angry and heartbroken. Your Building Team is merciful and patient. At exactly the right time, they expose every dark corner. In your sadness you might feel deserted or judged. The new Light is so bright that it takes a while to readjust your focus. During those transitional moments, you might feel rejected and alone. Have they abandoned you?

Not for a single second.

You learn a valuable lesson. One that you forget due to your sinful nature, and need to learn over and over again—your building is no more important or better than any other building that God is busy building.

There is only one thing keeping every single building standing: grace.

Grace meets everyone in the big aching gap. Grace gives everyone a new way out. Grace makes the way out possible. Grace provides every part of the discipleship process. It's by grace that nothing you do can make you lose the Christ Plan. Your identity is forever established in God's greater plan. Even when you make mistakes and sin, your Architect's oath remains for you to be built on the Christ Plan and to reach completion in eternity.

Where you might have thought that your spiritual building

would be maintained by actions that promote spiritual growth, you now realise differently.

Spiritual maintenance and grace are one and the same thing.

You will grow in faith and become mature throughout the discipleship process, but nothing is more powerful or important than clinging to God's grace. Our Architect makes sure that we stay humble (James 4:6).

It's not the amount of wisdom and knowledge about the Christ Plan that keep your living stones tightly together. It's the amount of grace that you receive and with which you build your entire building that determines its strength and stability.

God's grace is immeasurable and unlimited. It's available to every builder. Every builder decides how much grace they want to spread in between their stones. When you accept little grace for your own building, you will extend little grace at the buildings around you. Where grace is spread too thin, it's filled up with all the wrong reinforcements mentioned earlier.

Pride will cause you to justify your own actions and to look down at people who struggle. It will also deceive you into believing that your salvation and sanctification depends on yourself, and cause you to push the Holy Spirit as builder further away so you can follow your own agenda. Bitterness and unforgiveness towards yourself or others, don't reflect the heart of the Christ Plan. Comparison, ungratefulness, and jealousy jeopardizes the entire body, promoting even more pride and bitterness.

There certainly is a right and a wrong. There certainly is a fleshly, worldly plan versus the Christ Plan. We must be careful that we don't build according to the worldly *and* the Christ Plan *simultaneously.*

That mixed concrete is not pure and will never last. The mixed walls will be broken down continuously—for our good and for His glory. That is how grace maintains and sustains every building and the greater spiritual building as a whole.

The Christ Plan must always receive preference. That doesn't mean that we'll be looking around at everything that is explicitly wrong and just approve everything due to grace. To approve is not part of the Christ Plan. Jesus Christ didn't approve wrong things. We're responsible to help one another and to keep each other in the light of God's Word and truth. It's more about how we do it, than what we do.

Do we approach one another in love—and with grace—when we point out truth? Do we point out someone's faults and weaknesses to show that we know what is right or because we really want the best for them with all our hearts?

Jesus never judged anyone during His lifetime on earth. To the contrary He said: "I did not come to judge the world, but to save the world" (John 12:47, NIV). He did however warn and spoke sternly to the pharisees, who disregarded grace and relied on good works to try and attain righteousness.

After climbing Mount Kilimanjaro, one of my favourite authors, Hettie Brittz, wrote about the law versus grace. She says that all of us are surely burdened by the law and taken by life on impossible journeys and that she is starting to realise—if you're chosen by God's grace, to learn about grace—life will take you on one impossible journey after another, until you finally can't complete one of those journeys within your own might and power. Maybe it's not totally true that we choose grace—grace chooses us—but we choose how many mountains we want to climb before we hand ourselves over to grace.[10]

We also choose how many walls we want to build and break before we give ourselves completely over to God's grace.

---

[10] Brittz, H. *10 Gebooie van Genade. P.94*

Sanctifying Grace

Oh, God...
Mould and maintain me
For Your purpose and Your glory
Teach me and guide me
To not give in, but give over –
This weakness pressing on my shoulders
You seek pursuing, not perfection
Allowing process and even work in sections
You humble the proud –
No boasting of self allowed
For we are all sinners needing saving
No cross would lead to all decaying,
Unlimited grace for all who accept it
By faith alone and no good deed
You saved us by serving –
A people so undeserving,
You never stopped loving, never do:
Fully maintained by Your grace,
Until I finally come to You.
Amen

Summary

Remain in Him

You look back at that time of absolute brokenness, when the building rubble lay graceless around you, and the dust blew aimlessly about you. You remember how blinded you were and remember the aching gap. You remember everything that came out of that gap. You remember the darkness and loneliness. You remember your old way of building and the temporary coverups. All the efforts and building, all the trying and failing on your own, all the mistakes and breaking down...

Now, you look inwards. The gap is gone. The darkness and lies have been replaced with His light and truth. You are steadily anchored on the Rock. Your soul has found an everlasting resting place in Him as foundation. Your temporary walls have been replaced with an everlasting structure. You are being built up, in line with the Cornerstone. Every living stone that is laid down with the Holy Spirit, reveals something about God's mysterious Christ Plan. Even though you don't fully understand, you're not arguing against it anymore. You realise it has to do with a process and you're grateful for the time, opportunity, and grace that is provided to be part of it.

You realise that you're a stranger on earth and that you form part of a greater building. The Christ Plan will never fit into the worldly plan. There will be opposition because the world doesn't understand. Temptations and your own fleshly building plan, will always be present on this earth. The spiritual battle will always be fought. But you are not fighting alone, and you are not fighting without a purpose. You are fully geared and become more informed daily. You train daily and become spiritually stronger.

There will be days that you will celebrate—when solid walls are rounded off. There will also be days when you will need courage to rebuild crumbling walls. But now you understand that it's a lifelong process. You understand that your own agenda and ideas about perfection need to be discarded. You are not alone, not even for a moment. Even when the dust of life blind you and everything looks like a big mess, there's Someone with you. He holds all your living stones together. He holds all of us together. Only grace is keeping you standing, only grace is making this process possible. And grace means He never gives up, never withdraws, and never breaks His contract with you. His new covenant is everlasting and steadfast.

Even though you'll be building and breaking many more walls, and even though you'll be damaging many boundaries, He sees the lines of the Christ Plan in you. There's nothing you could ever do to destroy the Christ Plan.

Every day is a day closer to the final revealing day, when Jesus Christ will come and finally remove all the earthly dust from you. And in that moment that you fully enter His glory, you will fully see and fully understand, how you have always been built into Him and into the Father.

Amen.

Remain in You

Built on, into and for You:
Your true masterpiece image restored –
This temporary earthly temple transformed
As living stones connect
And reflect:
Grace covering all defects
Broken to be moulded,
The Christ Plan enfolded
And according to Your righteous plumb line
I'm washed and filled with living waters,
Enlightened to shine
To fill the gaps and repair the walls,
To sound the trumpet
And break down spiritual strongholds
New Cornerstone boundaries protect and guide –
No room for hardened hearts or fleshly pride
Saved by the Servant to serve
To love without limit or reserve
Each action building each living stone
Into His spiritual eternal home
His kingdom come –
A pattern of Heaven forming
A promise of everlasting morning dawning
So, press on, hold tight
Disciples closely following, not losing sight
Maintained and sustained by His Mercy
Until we finish the race
And the final capstone is placed:
Perfected and glorified
Forever free and worshipping, awe-inspired
Hallelujah! You are Holy!
Amen

There are not enough words to thank the following people. Thank you are two small words compared to the enormous impact you've had on my life and this book...

Thank you to my remarkable husband, Hannes. The value of your support, counsel, and unfailing love is immeasurable. Your trust in God's ways, and appreciation for His craftmanship enriches my own journey of faith in so many ways. I'm incredibly and humbly grateful for our marriage!

Thank you to my cherished children—this book is for you both. Johandré, you are so brave, wise beyond your years, detail oriented, and joyful. Vivia, you are so passionately creative, beautiful, loving, and vibrant. Without your loving presence and unique God-given designs, shaping my own heart and character, our lives' building plan, and this book, would never have reached its full potential. I pray you will always be passionate builders of God's kingdom.

Matthew, you are a super amazing nephew with such an amazing heart—may your light always shine. Marlia, and Anandie, you girls are spectacular. May the three of you understand your value and identity in Christ, and know you are also called for great things.

Thank you to my parents, André, and Sonja, as well as my brothers, Shaun, and Wynand, and my sister-in-law, Maret. Thank you for being part of my life's building process. God has an awe-inspiring way of creating masterpieces and a unique plan for each family. I love you dearly.

Thank you, mum, for going the extra mile and creating a masterpiece—capturing the vision of this book with your painting. It is one of my most treasured gifts.

Thank you to every precious fellow believer, pastor, life group member, and friend in my life, for your amazing friendship, prayers, and encouragement throughout my life, and this process. Thank you to my mother-in-law, Lynette, and granny, Suzie, that you are always interceding for our family members before God's throne. It's an enormous blessing to build this life alongside you all! I also *acknowledge granny Corrie, who's faith and prayers had paved a way for my own faith.*

You've each left a special and lasting imprint on my heart. Thank you...

Sources

Scripture used throughout the entire content:

Chapter 2: Preparation of the Construction Site & the Building Plan: A Heart Change

Yancey, P. Where is God When it Hurts? Copyright © 1990 by Phillip Yancey. Zondervan. p.35

Chapter 3: The Building Team (God): God as Architect, Jesus as the Building Plan, Holy Spirit as Builder

Dr. Simons, B. John. Eternal Love. The Passion Translation. Copyright © 2015 by BroadStreet Publishing Group, LLC. p.11

Chapter 4: God Our Rock, Christ Our Cornerstone

htttps://sahomes.in/blog/the-importance-of-strong-foundations-for-buildings/
Wohlman-Kon, H. DORleDOR. *The world Jewish Bible Society. Jerusalem. Building in Biblical Times. p.1*
https://www.merriam-webster.com/dictionary/cornerstone# synonyms

Chapter 5:

Hull, B. The Complete Book of Discipleship. On being and making followers of Christ. Copyright © 2006 by Robert W. Hull. Navpress Publishing Group. p.32

Piper, J. Don't waste your life. Copyright © 2003 by Desiring God Foundation. Text updated 2009. Reprinted with new cover 2018. Crossway is a publishing ministry of Good News Publishers. All rights reserved. p.66

Chapter 10: Spiritual Maintenance: Grace

Brittz, H. 10 Gebooie van genade. 'n Ekspedisie na vryheid. Copyright © 2015 by Green Hope Media. All rights reserved. p.94

Printed in the United States
By Bookmasters